INNER EXPERIENCES
OF EVOLUTION

Rudolf Steiner, Berlin (1910)

INNER EXPERIENCES OF EVOLUTION

Five Lectures Held in Berlin
October 31, 1911 – December 5, 1911

TRANSLATED BY JANN GATES
INTRODUCTION BY CHRISTOPHER BAMFORD

RUDOLF STEINER

SteinerBooks

CW 132

Copyright © 2009 by SteinerBooks

SteinerBooks
Anthroposophic Press

610 Main Street
Great Barrington, Massachusetts 01230
www.steinerbooks.org

Translation from the German by Jann Gates

This book is volume 132 in the Collected Works (CW) of Rudolf Steiner, published by SteinerBooks, 2009. It is a translation of the German *Die Evolution vom Gesichtspunkte des Wahrhaftigen*, published by Rudolf Steiner Verlag, Dornach, Switzerland, 1987.

Library of Congress Cataloging-in-Publication Data is available.

ISBN 978-0-88010-602-3

All rights reserved.
No part of this book may be reproduced in any form without written permission from the publisher, except for brief quotations embodied in critical articles for review.

CONTENTS

Introduction by Christopher Bamford   ix

1.

The Inner Aspect of the Saturn Embodiment of the Earth

BERLIN, OCTOBER 31, 1911

Ancient Saturn, Sun, and Moon existences work into the present time. Fear and terror at the sight of ancient Saturn's endless void is overcome through inner firmness and certainty. An echo of this in the journals of Karl Rosenkranz. The Gospels and Anthroposophy as support for bearing the experience of the terrifying void of ancient Saturn. Encountering the Spirits of Will (Thrones) as a surging sea of courage. The absence of time and space on ancient Saturn. From the sacrifice brought by the Spirits of Will to the Cherubim, time is born. All outer warmth today is maya (illusion); it is the outer semblance, the reflection of the sacrifice of the Spirits of Will to the Cherubim. An imagination: the Spirits of Will kneeling with complete devotion and courage before the Cherubim, offering flaming warmth out of which the Spirits of Time emerge. The impossibility of understanding this image of ancient Saturn through intellectual philosophy. Albert Schwegler and Jacob Boehme.

pages 1–13

2.

The Inner Aspect of the Sun Embodiment of the Earth

BERLIN, NOVEMBER 7, 1911

Recapitulation of the spiritual activity that occurred on ancient Saturn. The ancient Sun stage adds air and light. Air is an illusion; what we experience as air in external reality is the result of the archetypal act of bestowing their own being by the Spirits of Wisdom. The act of giving as a creative activity; association of air with creative ability. An imagination: the sacrificing Thrones kneeling before the Cherubim; choirs of the Spirits of Wisdom surrendering in devotion to the vision of the sacrifice of the Thrones at the center of the Sun, their devotion growing into an image of sacrificial smoke; the Archangels being created out of the smoke and radiating the gift of the sacrificial smoke back from the periphery in the form of light. Archangels preserve the recollection of the archetypal beginnings. The role of the Christ impulse in Earth evolution; the *Last Supper* by Leonardo da Vinci as a true expression of this.

pages 14–28

3.

The Inner Aspect of the Sun Embodiment of the Earth and the Transition to the Moon Embodiment

BERLIN, NOVEMBER 14, 1911

Creative resignation leads to spiritual results in higher worlds. Luciferic beings remained behind during the course of development on ancient Moon. The achievement of eternity and immortality through the renunciation of the sacrifice of the Spirits of Will by some of the Cherubim: the separation of time and eternity. The coming into being of water on ancient Moon. Water as a substance is illusion; it is a reflection of the renunciation by the Spirits of Will of what they could have received from the Cherubim. The rejected sacrifice-substance is taken hold of by the luciferic beings, and through this, opposition, evil, comes into being. The sacrifice of Isaac as a picture of God's forgoing a sacrifice. Leonardo's *Last Supper* as a picture of Christ's renunciation by taking Judas into the circle of the apostles.

pages 29–45

4.

The Inner Aspect of the Moon Embodiment of the Earth

BERLIN, NOVEMBER 21, 1911

The mood of longing comes into being in the Spirits of Will whose sacrifice the Cherubim forgo. Cain's confrontation with Abel personifies in an extreme way some of the meaning of "rejected sacrifice." The lighting up of egoism through the will to sacrifice that has been held back. The appearance of the Spirits of Movement, which brings change into the cosmos as partial satisfaction of the longing of the Spirits of Will. Spiritual science as a response to longings in the subconscious. The tragedy of Heinrich von Kleist.

pages 46–61

5.
The Inner Aspect of the Earth Embodiment of the Earth

BERLIN, DECEMBER 5, 1911

Finding the truth behind outer world manifestations by taking soul experiences as the starting point. Healthy knowledge arises through wonder and the delight that solving a riddle engenders. The concept of astonishment. The melancholic character of ancient Moon development as the result of the rejected sacrifice of the Spirits of Will. Cain's sacrifice points symbolically to the starting point for the evolution of earthly humankind. The alienation of the substance of sacrifice from its origin: death. The true nature of the earth or solid element is death, that which has been alienated from its meaning through rejection. Death in relation to the mineral, plant, and animal. Human beings must achieve "I"-consciousness in the physical context; it cannot be found without death; only human beings can experience death. Conquering of death through Christ. An archetype of this event does not exist in the spiritual world; it could only occur on Earth. Attaining an understanding of the Mystery of Golgotha is possible only on Earth. Experience of the etheric Christ by Paul at Damascus and the experience of perceiving Christ through higher capacities by ever more people starting in the twentieth century. A story demonstrating the difference between what is arithmetically correct and what is actually true: the relationship of science to truth.

pages 62–78

Reference Notes 79
Rudolf Steiner's Collected Works 85
Significant Events in the Life of Rudolf Steiner 101
Index 115

INTRODUCTION

Christopher Bamford

One of the most remarkable aspects of Rudolf Steiner's life is how, as a spiritual researcher, he is able continuously to deepen and expand our understanding of the inner meaning of the reality from and into which we are born—that in which, as St. Paul put it, "we live and move and have our being." A reader, faced with the almost impossible number of lectures and lecture cycles that seem to flow in an ever-expanding series, may be forgiven for thinking that many of them—to some extent at least—must be repetitions. Certainly, within any short given period, there may be a theme that Steiner is researching and on which he will report a number of times. But even when the theme is the same, and the instances where this is so are in fact quite rare, there is seldom exact repetition, but always something new, because, for the most part, the lectures present not ready-made teaching or answers, but reports of ongoing meditative research. In every lecture and lecture course, Rudolf Steiner is setting himself a challenge, giving himself the task of going deeper into a question and find something new. This is what makes reading him so exciting.

The year 1911 is no exception in this. In response to the broadening split in the Theosophical Society occasioned by promotion of the young Krishnamurti as the "Messiah," Rudolf Steiner refined the anthroposophical work, giving a series of critical lecture courses, each in its own way marking a quantum leap in understanding and exposition. The specific theme, if there was one, was evolution and the need to understand humanity today from within, and the present human task as evolving out of the seed ground of the universe. Doing so, required on the one hand deepening the esoteric basis of Anthroposophy, while at the same time elaborating the methodology of consciousness that made it possible. At the heart of both endeavors stands the Christic Mystery, the "turning point of time," the realization of which not only the future of humanity but also the entirety of cosmic evolution hangs.

Thus, the year 1911 began with the last lecture of the cycle *Occult History in the Light of Anthroposophy*, and led into individual public lectures on "turning points"—incarnated by such figures as Zarathustra, Hermes, Moses, and Buddha—marking the evolutionary stages leading up to the Christ event. Then, in March, in Prague, Steiner gave the unique series of lectures *Occult Physiology*, while in April he attended the Fourth International Congress of Philosophy in Bologna, Italy, where he delivered his seminal methodological paper "The Psychological Foundations and the Epistemological Position of Theosophy (Anthroposophy)." In June, in Denmark, he addressed the overall theme of the year in a short series of lectures that, written up, would be printed as *The Spiritual Guidance of the Individual and Humanity*. Summer then saw the premiere of his second Mystery Drama, *The Soul's Probation*, followed by the extraordinary cycle on Greek mythology as it leads to and through the Christ event, *Wonders of the World, Trials of the Soul, Spirit Revelations*. In October, as if coming to some conclusion, Steiner addressed his theme head-on in the epochal cycle *From Jesus to Christ*. Then, as if to conclude, or place them within the larger context, he followed with the lectures printed here. And the year came to an end with the lectures "Pneumatosophy" (published in *A Psychology of Body, Soul, and Spirit*) and *The World of the Senses and the World of the Spirit* (December). Scattered throughout the year were also lectures on the mission of Christian Rosenkreutz, as well as other single lectures on different aspects of evolution.

The foundations for all this work were laid in the previous decade (as well as the two preparatory decades leading up to Steiner's uniting his destiny and spiritual mission with the Theosophical Society.) The so-called "basic books," especially *Theosophy* and *An Outline of Esoteric Science* sketched out what would then later be continuously amplified. Ongoing research, reported in lectures, such as the great Gospel cycles and the various lectures on the "etheric Christ," the Archangel Michael, and the different spiritual hierarchies, filled out the picture with details hardly dreamed of earlier. By 1911, the groundwork was finished. There remained the hard work of building upon it, and discovering a more natural, more phenomenological, and appropriate language, less reliant on jargon. It was time to go deeper, approach reality from the inside, from the side of experience, rather than outwardly and quasi-schematically.

And so, almost it feels slipped in between other engagements, we have these five unique, moving lectures on some deeply felt "glimpses of the truth" that evolution inwardly experienced can give us. Many times over the years, Steiner had unfolded the magnificent, dynamic picture of the Earth's organic and successive evolution as an alchemical process. He had described many times, always adding something, how, passing through the progressive metamorphoses he calls the Saturn, Sun, and Moon stages or existences, we have arrived at Earth and Earth-consciousness—itself but a stage in a still evolving process. Up to this point, he had always described the stages more or less from the *outside*. Now, however, he will begin to hint as to their *inner* experience, directing us toward their inner meaning as we can experience it today. Indeed, as he says, although these "past" stages have left an impression that may be read in the so-called Akashic substance, whatever "was once set into the stream of time continues to come to fruition even today." That is, these stages are present and available in their consequences in the world we see.

He begins with the Saturn stage as the environment or world (such words are only approximate) in which the true "I" lives. For the world of the "I" and the world of Saturn are the same. As Steiner says, "If we tried to discover the essential context for the 'I' in the same sense as we know the context for the physical body, then we would come to a cosmic portrait or tableau that invisibly permeates our surroundings even today and is identical to the cosmic tableau of ancient Saturn."

To begin to experience this state, we must, as it were, shed all sensory reality, and leave behind our "inner life." Ordinary thinking, feeling, and willing must cease until in that silence nothing exists, only the essential human being we are. Where then are we? We are in a void, an absolute dimensionless emptiness, without time and space. There is at first no orientation, clearly a terrifying experience, one full of horror and vertigo. Our consciousness feels frozen.

Only the virtues of Christ (Steiner says), which are taught also by Anthroposophy—trust, gratitude, love, and the dedication to serve—can get us through. Upheld by these, we sense "courage" approaching. It is the presence of the Thrones, the Spirits of Will. Simultaneously there is a differentiation, a glow, a presentiment of wisdom or intelligence streaming in—the Cherubim. And, finally, the sense that the Thrones, the Spirits of Will, are sacrificing their being to the Cherubim. And time then in a certain sense arises—not abstract time, but Time Beings, the Archai—and also warmth, the "same" warmth we know today. Such is the world of the "I," but also such still resounds in the warmth of the world we live in. Working with it both meditatively and imaginally, we can begin to enter into and participate in it.

The "atmosphere" of the Saturn state has clearly something moral about it, and this sense that the cosmos is moral becomes sharper as we enter the Sun stage. Here two new qualities appear. There is a sense of enlivening bliss—the happiness one experiences witnessing a beautiful deed, that is, the kind of feeling one would experience if one witnessed the sacrifice of the Thrones. And within the joy, in a way both simultaneous with it and making it possible, a feeling of surrender, dedication, and deep devotion arises. Without such self-surrender and deep receptivity, Steiner says, no spiritual experience—no spiritual gift or illumination from the gift-giving Spirits of Wisdom—is possible.

Giving—or "bestowing"—and receiving characterize the qualities of the Sun state. Entering deeply into them, we can begin to comprehend the true meaning of air and light, and of the beings—the Spirits of Wisdom and the Archangels, Messengers of the Beginning—whose primal activity still lives in our world today. For giving and receiving in the Sun stage begin to make possible the unfolding, the separating, of inner and outer: that is, the creation of space. Space thus begins to appear, but at first in only two dimensions, a circle inwardly illuminated. Here, too, the Christ Being originates, resuming in the purest way the innermost moral qualities radiating within the sphere.

Something else is also characteristic of the Sun state, another inner quality or virtue, which Steiner calls "will," but not will as we usually (and perhaps wrongly) conceive of it. We usually think of will as a kind of inner strength or positive, active power of conscious intention that we develop. This, following Georg Kühlewind, we could call the "hard" will. It is what we use to roll a boulder up a hill. The other will, which Kühlewind calls "soft," Steiner characterizes with the word "renunciation," saying:

> To accomplish the greatest deeds, to achieve the greatest results in the spiritual world...a certain resignation, a renunciation, is needed.

So we too must learn to renounce, just as certain of the spiritual beings in the Sun state "renounced" their tasks. Their renunciation gave rise to "water." "Water," Steiner says, "arises out of resignation; in fact, water actually is resignation." The other side of "water" is immortality, or eternity. So, with renunciation not only "water" arises, but also time divides into flowing time and eternity. And not only that: by their renunciation these "luciferic" beings, who, in a way, sacrificed themselves and held themselves back, and thereby opened the possibility of "evil," by the same deed provided the space for human freedom. "The gods had to allow evil to come into the world for the sake of human freedom, and therefore they also had to acquire the strength necessary to lead evil back to the good. And this capacity is something that can come about only as a consequence of renunciation and resignation."

We see this power of renunciation above all in Christ, who accepted Judas into his sphere and submitted to the Cross: "Not my will but thy will be done."

From this "inner" picture of the Saturn and Sun stages of evolution, we thus begin to see that behind earthly qualities such as warmth (heat or fire), air, and water lie profound spiritual deeds of sacrifice, giving (or bestowing), and renunciation or resignation. In fact, these apparently earthly substances are the *expression* of these spiritual deeds, available to us through meditative perceiving as spiritual faculties or gestures.

Moving next to the Moon stage, Steiner begins by focusing on the inner experience of one whose sacrifice is apparently "rejected," as God rejects Cain's sacrifice. I say apparently, because there was nothing wrong with Cain's offering—there was no "fault or failure" on his part. God simply "withdrew his acceptance." Often, as in the case of Cain, this experience can give rise to feelings not so much of opposition, injustice, as of unfulfilled yearning or, perhaps better put, unconditional yearning (a "will that cannot be realized'). All of us can, if we are honest, find such feelings in the depths of our soul life.

Such anyway was what the beings whose sacrifice was rejected experienced: their wills were restrained, they were held back, but still open. And from this experience, something like "egoity" arose. As Steiner puts it:

> Within longing we see egoism flashing like lightning, albeit in its weakest form; and we also see longing slipping into cosmic development. And thus we see how beings who surrender to longing, that is, surrender themselves to their egoism are—if something else does not intervene—condemned in a certain way to one-sidedness, to living merely in themselves.

In the Moon stage, the Spirits of Movement intervened. They made it possible for new relationships—relationships to others—to be formed. And with relationships, picture consciousness—a soul life of images—arose as a healing balm for the unsatisfied longing. Desolation, egoic pain and torment were thus overcome: connection was possible.

Steiner goes on to show that if the Moon is the "planet of longing," then the Earth is the "planet of redemption." However, as the planet of redemption, it is, by the same token and for that very reason, the planet of death. Using the language of the elements, we can say that we have seen the arising of the cosmic-spiritual elements of fire, air, and water. The element that remains to arise is earth. Earth, Steiner says, in a sense means not to stand in one's own place. The earthly fact of death that only human beings experience is evidence, in fact, that, as human beings, we do not stand in our own place.

How did death arise on Earth? The beings whose sacrifice was rejected felt "excluded" from their cosmic meaning and purpose. They felt "torn out" of the process: alienated from their origins. "If one understands this sensitively," Steiner says,

> If one places sensitively before one's soul this idea of something in which alienation from its origins dwells—then one has the idea of death.... And the true meaning of death is nothing other than the state of not being in one's true place, of being excluded from one's true place.

Thus, the fourth element in the universe, earth, is death. On Earth, death exists for human beings—and only for them—as something real and in its own right. Death is the only earthly reality that is not maya. It is truly and spiritually real. As Steiner says: *"In the Mystery of Golgotha we have something that belongs immediately and directly to the world of reality."* This is what makes Christ's deed so central and why it had to occur on Earth, the only place death is. By Christ's overcoming of death, Christ now shines forth in death itself. Death is transformed. The Earth is transformed. And the gods also, for no god had ever known death before. And yet, paradoxically, this event—the Mystery of Golgotha—in a sense the only real spiritual-physical event on Earth, can be cognized and perceived only spiritually. It left no traces perceivable by outer observation. It is indeed remarkable, as Steiner concludes

> that this event, which occurred on the outer physical plane, shares a common characteristic with all facts of the supersensible realm: namely that it does not allow itself to be proven in any outward way. And many of those people who deny the supersensible world are the same ones who lack the capacity to grasp this event—which is not at all a supersensible one. In fact, the reality of the event is supported by the effects it produces. Yet people suppose these events can occur without the real event itself actually having occurred historically. They explain that the effects are a consequence of sociological circumstances. But for someone who is familiar with the course of cosmic creation, the

idea that the effects of Christianity could have occurred without a force standing behind them is about as clever as saying that cabbages can grow in a field without planting seeds.

For anyone interested in what Steiner calls "the course of cosmic creation," this humble little book will be a treasure of untold insights, worthy of long and deep meditation.

INNER EXPERIENCES
OF EVOLUTION

Rudolf Steiner

1

The inner Aspect of the Saturn Embodiment of the Earth

BERLIN, OCTOBER 31, 1911

If we wish to continue to explore the reflections we worked on last year in our branch evenings, we shall have to master some concepts, ideas, and perceptions other than those we have spoken of so far.† For what we have to say about the Gospels and the other spiritual documents of humankind would not by itself be enough, unless we presume the development of our entire cosmic system. We have described this evolution as the embodiment of our planet itself through Saturn, Sun, and Moon existences up to the present Earth existence. Whoever remembers how often we have referred to these fundamental principles also knows how necessary they are for all esoteric observations concerning human evolution.† However, if you look at the account of the developmental stages of Saturn, Sun, Moon, and Earth described in *An Outline of Esoteric Science*, you will have to admit that what is given there is only a sketch—even if it had been expanded, it would not be otherwise. It is only a sketch from a certain point of view so that an explanation could then be given from a particular perspective. For just as Earth existence offers an immense wealth of details, so, too, it stands to reason, there are likewise an endless number of details to record about the Saturn, Sun, and Moon existences. Even so, it is always only possible to give a "rough sketch" or "outline" of these details. In these lectures, then, we shall have to portray a characteristic of evolution from yet another side.

When we ask ourselves where all of these accounts originate, we know that they come from so-called entries in the Akashic Chronicle.† We know that whatever once occurred in the course of cosmic development may, to some extent, be read by means of an impression in a delicate spiritual substance called the Akasha substance. Everything that has happened has left an imprint of this kind from which one can elicit how things once were. In the physical world, when we look at something, we can assume that things nearer to us are generally clear and distinct in their details, and that the farther away things are, the less clear and distinct they appear. Things that are closer to us in time also reveal themselves more exactly than things that are farther removed in time. It is the same when we look back in a supersensible sense: the Saturn or Sun existences, for example, will have less distinct outlines than the Earth or Moon periods of development.

But why do this at all? Why do we consider it important to "track down" a time that lies so far distant from our own? Someone might well ask: "Why do these anthroposophists bring up these ancient matters today? We certainly do not need to concern ourselves with such things. We have enough to do with what is going on in the present."

It would be wrong to speak in such a way. For what was once set into the stream of time continues to come to fruition even today. What was brought into being in the time of Saturn development did not exist simply and exclusively in and for that era. What occurred then continues to affect our time, but it has become veiled and invisible in relation to what exists externally in the physical plane around human beings. Indeed, what occurred so long ago during ancient Saturn existence is barely visible today. Nevertheless, ancient Saturn existence is still significant for humankind. In order to imagine why it is significant for us, let us place the following before our soul.

We know that the innermost core of our being stands before us as what we call the "I." This "I," the innermost core of our being, is truly an immaterial, imperceptible entity for humanity today. Just how imperceptible it is can be inferred from what is said about the soul in the so-called "official" psychologies. These no longer have any notion of what constitutes the being of the "I," or, indeed, that such an "I" may even be intimated.

I have often drawn attention to the fact that, in nineteenth century German psychology, the expression "soul theory without soul" gradually came into use. The world-famous school of Wilhelm Wundt,[†] which is influential not just in German-speaking countries, but is greatly respected wherever psychology is discussed, made this "soul theory without soul" fashionable.[†] This "soul theory without soul" describes soul qualities without presupposing an independent soul entity. Instead, all qualities of the soul first come together in a kind of focal point, that is, gather themselves in the "I." That is the greatest absurdity that has ever been linked to a theory about the soul. Yet psychology today stands completely under its influence; today, this notion is celebrated throughout the world. Cultural historians studying our era in the future will have their work cut out for them if they wish to explain plausibly how such a theory could ever have been regarded as the greatest achievement in the field of psychology in the nineteenth century and well into the twentieth. I say this only to point out how unclear "official" psychology is with regard to the "I," the middle point of the human being.

If we could grasp the "I" in its true nature and set it before us in the way we can set the physical body before us, and then tried to discover the environment upon which the "I" depends—in the sense that the physical body depends upon what is seen outwardly by the eyes and perceived through the senses, and needs nourishment, and discovers clouds, mountains, and so forth, in its surroundings in the physical realm—that is, if we tried to discover the essential context for the "I" in the same sense as we know the context for the physical body, then we would come to a cosmic portrait or tableau that invisibly permeates our surroundings even today and is identical to the cosmic tableau of ancient Saturn. In other words, whoever wishes to come to know the "I" in its world must be able to imagine a world like that of ancient Saturn. This world is hidden; it is a world that is, for human beings, beyond sense perception. Indeed, at our present level of development, we cannot bear the perception of it. The Guardian of the Threshold veils it from us.[†] It thus remains concealed—for a certain level of spiritual development is required to withstand the sight of such a tableau.

In fact, the sight of such a tableau as ancient Saturn presents is one to which a person must first become accustomed. Before anything else, you must form an imagination of how one could ever experience such a cosmic tableau as something real. All that you perceive with the senses must be removed from your thinking. Also, insofar as it consists of the usual ebb and flow within the soul, you must abandon your inner world. You must erase thinking about what is in the world—and even dissolve all ideas themselves. You must remove from the outer world everything perceived through the senses; you must extinguish the activity of the soul and of ideas within your inner world. Having done this, if you wish to form an idea of the soul condition that must be reached if a human being is really to grasp this thought—remember, absolutely everything is removed, only the human being remains—then one can only say that you must be able to bear the terror, the fear of the fathomless void, the endless emptiness, that yawns around us. One must be capable of experiencing an environment completely saturated with fear and terror and yet, at one and the same time, be able to overcome these feelings through the inner firmness and certainty of one's own being. Without these two dispositions in the soul—the terror of an infinite void of existence and the overcoming of this fear—you cannot possibly experience any inkling of how ancient Saturn existence underlies our cosmic existence.

People, on their own, seldom cultivate the two experiences that I have just characterized. One also finds very little that has been written about this condition. Of course, those who, over the course of time, have tried to explore it with clairvoyant forces know of it. Yet, there are very few indications in written or published sources, that people have experienced either this terror before an infinite abyss or the overcoming of this fear.

In order to gain some insight into this matter, I investigated recent literature in which something like this terror in the face of an immeasurable void appeared. Philosophers are usually very clever, speaking knowledgeably about concepts, but completely avoid mentioning awe-inspiring impressions. So one does not easily find something recorded in philosophical literature about this matter. I will not speak now of sources where I found nothing. But once I did find an echo of these experiences in the journal of the Hegelian philosopher, Karl Rosenkranz.† In this journal, Rosenkranz described very intimate feelings that he had experienced while immersing himself in Hegelian philosophy. I came across a remarkable passage that he recorded quite innocently in his journal. It was clear to Rosenkranz that Hegelian philosophy is based on Hegel's understanding of "pure being." In the philosophical literature of the nineteenth century there has been a great deal of superficial talk about Hegel's principle of "pure being"— but, in fact, it is very poorly understood. One can almost say that philosophy in the second half of the nineteenth century understands about as much about Hegel's "pure being" as an ox understands about Sunday when he has been munching fodder the whole week through! Hegel's concept of "pure being"—not the process of being, but the state of being as such—is not quite what I characterized as the dreaded emptiness into which fear flows, but all of space in Hegel's "being" is tinged with a quality that cannot be experienced by humankind: the Infinite filled with Being. And Karl Rosenkranz once experienced this as the dreadful, shattering state of the coldness of the cosmic expanse of space devoid of content other than sheer being.

To grasp what lies at the basis of the cosmos, it is not enough to speak about it merely in concepts or to make up ideas about it. It is much more important to call up an imagination of what one experiences facing the infinite void that characterizes ancient Saturn existence. Then the soul grasps the feeling of horror, even if only an inkling of it. One can prepare oneself to behold this Saturn condition clairvoyantly by replicating the feeling of vertigo in mountain heights, of standing at the edge of an abyss without a secure footing, of being driven from one place to the next, overwhelmed by forces over which one no longer has any influence. That is the first step, the initial feeling. Then one loses not just the ground under one's feet, but what the eyes see, the ears hear, the hands can grasp—absolutely everything that exists in the surrounding space. And, inevitably, one loses every thought, plunging into a kind of twilight or sleep state in which one cannot grasp anything cognitively. Or else—one immerses oneself into every feeling, and then nothing else is possible but to slip into a condition of dread, often gripped by a state of dizziness that cannot be overcome.

There are two possibilities for human beings today to overcome the grip of fear at the abyss. One established way is through an understanding of the Gospels, through an understanding of the Mystery of Golgotha. A person who truly understands the Gospels—not in the way modern theologians speak about them, but who absorbs the very deepest of what can be experienced inwardly of the Gospels—takes something with him or her into the abyss that expands as if from a single point and completely fills the void with a feeling of courage, of being protected through a union with the being who consummated the sacrifice at Golgotha. That is one way. The other way is to penetrate the spiritual worlds without the Gospels but with true, authentic Anthroposophy. That, too, is possible. As you know, I always emphasize that, when we consider the Mystery of Golgotha, we do not begin with the Gospels—for we would discover the Mystery of Golgotha even if there were no Gospels. This is something that was not possible *before* the Mystery of Golgotha occurred, but it is so today, because through the Mystery of Golgotha something came into the world that allows human beings to grasp the spiritual world directly out of impressions from the spiritual world. We may call this the presence of the Holy Spirit in the world, the rule of cosmic thoughts in the world. But one must be prepared.

If, when we must face the terrifying void, we take either the Gospels or Anthroposophy with us, then we cannot get lost nor plunge into the infinite abyss. If we approach this ghastly void with the preparation set forth in *How to Know Higher Worlds* (and the other works following it),† and penetrate the spiritual world—where everything that arises convulses our feelings and seizes our thoughts—we will meet beings who are not at all like those in the realms of animal, plant, or mineral. As we become familiar with and adjusted to Saturn existence, a world in which there are no clouds, no light, no sound, we will come to know beings. Indeed, we will come to know the beings who, in our terminology, are called the Spirits of Will or the

Thrones. These Spirits of Will whom we come to know as an objective reality, comprise, so to speak, a surging sea of courage.

What human beings at first can only imagine becomes objective *presence* through clairvoyance. Think of yourself immersed in the sea, and yet immersed in it as a spiritual being who feels united with the Christ Being, upheld by the Christ Being, swimming, but now not in a sea of water but in a sea that completely fills an infinite expanse and consists of flowing courage, surging energy! This is not simply an indifferent, undifferentiated sea. All possibilities and varieties of what we may describe as the feeling of courage come to meet us there. There we become acquainted with beings who consist of courage, yet are also quite individualized. Although they are made up entirely of courage, we encounter them also as concrete beings. Naturally it seems very strange to say that one meets beings who are as real as human beings composed of flesh, but who consist of courage not flesh. But this is so. We encounter the Spirits of Will who are beings of just this sort, and, meeting them, we thereby describe Saturn existence—for that is precisely what the Spirits of Will, composed of courage, represent. This is Saturn. It is a world that is not shaped like a sphere; it does not have six corners or four corners. Aspects of space do not apply. Thus there is no possibility of finding an "end" to Saturn existence. If we wanted to use the image of swimming again, we could say that Saturn is a sea that has no surface. Instead, everywhere, in every direction, Spirits of Courage or Spirits of Will are to be found.

I will characterize in later lectures how it is that one does not come to this insight immediately. For now I am going to use the sequence I used before: Saturn, Sun, Moon. It is actually better to go in the opposite direction—in the way that it is actually perceived clairvoyantly, namely, from Earth to Saturn. But for now I shall characterize it as: Saturn, Sun, Moon. The sequence in itself makes no difference.

The unique thing about it is that when one lifts oneself to this vision, something arises that is extremely difficult to imagine if one has not taken care to arrive at the ideas slowly and deliberately. For something ceases to exist that is more intimately tied to the ordinary capacity of imagination than anything else: *space ceases to exist.* There is no longer any meaning to expressions such as: one swims "on top of," or "underneath," "in front of," or "behind," "to the right" or "to the left"—or indeed any other similar reference to spatial relationships. In ancient Saturn, spatial relationships make no sense at all. "Everywhere" is the "same." But the most important thing is that when one enters the first periods of Saturn existence, time also ceases. There is simply no earlier or later. That is naturally very difficult for human beings today to imagine, because today a person's ideas themselves flow within time: one thought appears before or after another one. The absence of time, however, may be approximated through a feeling. But this feeling is not a pleasant one.

Imagine that your capacity for forming ideas is paralyzed so that everything that enables you to remember, everything you plan to do, becomes paralyzed like a rigid rod. Thus you feel as if your ideas are held fast and you can no longer touch them. In this condition you cannot say that something you experienced "before" happened at an "earlier" point in time. You are connected to it, it is there, but it is absolutely fixed. Time has ceased to have any meaning. It absolutely does not exist. Therefore, it is meaningless to ask: "Now that you have described the Saturn and Sun existences and so forth, can you tell me what was there before the Saturn existence?" "Before" has no meaning in that context. Time did not exist then, and we must do without any designations relating to time. Saturn existence is similar to a situation in which the world has been boarded up. Thoughts have come to a standstill. This is the case for clairvoyance, too. Normal thoughts have been left behind; they do not reach that far. Expressed pictorially: your brain is frozen. To the extent that you can perceive this state of paralysis, you can approximate the image of a consciousness that no longer encompasses time.

Having come this far, one notices a remarkable change occurring in the whole picture. Beings of other hierarchies penetrate and become active within the paralysis that is the timelessness of the infinite ocean of courage with its Spirits of Will. At the very moment when the absence of time is evident, one notices the activity of other beings. One notices the presence of something within the infinite ocean of courage, but with unspecified awareness. It is as if one did not experience it. Something lights up this expanse—but it is more like a glow than a quick flash of lightning. It is the first differentiation—a glow, but not a glow that gives the impression of a glowing light.

You must try to comprehend these things in different ways. For example, you might imagine something like the following: You meet someone who speaks to you, and you have the feeling, "How intelligent this person is!" And as the person continues to speak, this feeling intensifies, and you recognize, "This person is wise, has experienced the infinite, and thus is able to recount wise things." Furthermore, this person makes you feel as if he or she exuded an aura of enchantment. Imagine, then, this element of enchantment infinitely intensified. Imagine that in the ocean of courage, clouds appear in which there are not exactly flashes of lightning but shimmering radiance. When you take all of this together, you have an imagination of the beings now active within the Spirits of Will, beings who are not merely wisdom, but radiant streams of wisdom. You have here an idea of what, by means of clairvoyant perception, the Cherubim are. The Cherubim are the beings who stream into the ocean of courage.

Now imagine that nothing else surrounds you except what I have described. Actually, as I emphasized earlier, you cannot say that you have something "around" you. You can only say it is "there." You have to think your way into it. Now the image of something lighting up is not quite accurate. For this reason I said that it is not like a flash but more like a glowing—for everything occurs at the same time. It is not something that comes into being at one moment and disappears at another. Everything is simultaneous. Nevertheless, one has a feeling of a connection between the Spirits of Will and the Cherubim. One has the feeling that they established a relationship one to another. This becomes a conscious awareness. And one also becomes conscious that the Spirits of Will, the Thrones, sacrifice their own beings to the Cherubim. That is the final image one receives moving backward toward Saturn. One receives the image of the Spirits of Will directing this sacrifice to the Cherubim. Beyond this point it is as if the cosmos were "boarded up."

But to the extent that we experiences this sacrifice of the Spirits of Will to the Cherubim, something is pressed out of—separated—from our being. We can express this with the words: From the sacrifice brought by the Spirits of Will to the Cherubim, *time is born*. But this time is not abstract time, as we usually speak of it; it is an independent being. Only at this point can we speak of something beginning. Time initially is a time being, a being made up entirely of time. Beings are born, who consist only of time. These are the Spirits of Personality, whom we know as Archai in the hierarchy of spiritual beings. In Saturn existence, the Archai are entirely time. We have also described them as "Time Spirits"—as spirits who order time. They are born as spirits, but they are actually beings who consist entirely of time.

It is extraordinarily important to participate in the sacrifice of the Spirits of Will to the Cherubim and in the birth of the Spirits of Time. Only after time is born does something else emerge that allows us to speak about the Saturn condition as if it were something similar to what now surrounds us. What we call the element of warmth in Saturn is the sacrificial smoke of the Thrones, which generates time. I have always said that Saturn exists as a state of warmth. In doing so, I have described what exists there. For, among all of the elements we have around us at present, we can identify only warmth as an element that also existed in ancient Saturn. Warmth was generated out of the sacrifice that the Spirits of Will presented to the Cherubim. This also shows us how we should think about fire. Where we see fire, where we feel warmth, we should not think about it materialistically, as human beings today naturally and customarily do. Rather, wherever we see warmth, wherever we feel warmth, that is still today the sacrifice of the Spirits of Will to the Cherubim. Even though the spiritual foundation of warmth is invisible in our surroundings, it nonetheless exists. Through this insight the world arrives at the truth that, behind each manifestation of warmth, stands a sacrifice.

In *An Outline of Esoteric Science* mostly only the outer condition of ancient Saturn was described, to avoid offending people too much. Even that caused offense. Those who can think only in current scientific terms regard the book as pure nonsense. But think what it means, if a person could actually say:

- Ancient Saturn had at its innermost being, at its very foundation, beings belonging to the Spirits of Will who sacrificed themselves to the Cherubim.
- Out of the smoke generated by the sacrifice of the Spirits of Will to the Cherubim, time was born.
- Out of the birth of time, the Archai or the Time Spirits were sent forth.
- Warmth, as we know it, is the outer semblance, the reflection, of the sacrifice of the Spirits of Will.
- Now, outer warmth is an illusion (maya). If we wish to speak the truth, it is: wherever warmth is manifest, we have, in truth, sacrifice—the sacrifice of the Thrones before the Cherubim.

Cultivating the capacity of imagination is the second stage of Rosicrucian initiation. (This is mentioned often in *How to Know Higher Worlds* and elsewhere.) Anthroposophists must form imaginations out of sound representations of the world. In this way we can transform thinking into fantasy-imbued imagination. We can take, for example, what we have spoken of today. The Thrones or Spirits of Will kneel before the Cherubim with complete devotion that arises not out of a feeling of insignificance but out of the consciousness that they have something that they can sacrifice. The Thrones in this willingness to sacrifice, which is based upon strength and courage, kneel before the Cherubim and offer up their sacrifice to them. The Thrones send the sacrifice forth as effervescent warmth, flaming warmth, so that the smoke from the fire of sacrifice blazes upward to the winged Cherubim! So may we picture this reality. And now, arising from this sacrifice, as if we were speaking a word into the air and this word were time, but time as *beings*—from the totality of these occurrences—the Spirits of Time or the Archai emerge. This sending forth of the Archai is a powerful image. And this image, placed before our soul, is extremely potent for certain imaginations that can bring us ever deeper into the realms of hidden knowledge.

This transformation of the ideas we receive into imaginations, pictures, is what we must accomplish. Even if the pictures we make are primitive, even if they are anthropomorphic, even if these beings we try to portray look like winged persons—that is beside the point. It doesn't matter. Whatever needs to be added to our efforts will eventually be given to us. What our imaginations should not have will disappear. If we simply allow ourselves to be immersed in such pictures, that activity itself will actually guide us to such beings.

If you can accept this attempt to characterize courage-filled beings, overflowing with wisdom, you will see that the soul must soon turn to all manner of pictures that are remote from concepts formed by reason. Intellectual concepts came into existence much later. We ought not to approach the Saturn existence, in any case, in a purely intellectual way. You must come to understand what it means for clairvoyance to unfold in a person's mind: someone who describes something out of naive clairvoyance portrays it differently than a person who is intellectually oriented. An intellectual for his or her part never properly understands such minds. I want to give you an example of this. Take Albert Schwegler's (1819-1857) *History of Philosophy* (Stuttgart, 1848), a book that students used to like to study before taking their examinations but which, since the soul has been removed from philosophy, is no longer useful.† Even though the book has suffered from revisions in later editions, what was important in the original has not been entirely lost. This book is a history of philosophy from the Hegelian perspective. Thus you can take Schwegler's *History of Philosophy*, and you will have a good picture of philosophy in general at the time it was written and an excellent source on Hegelian philosophy. But now read the short chapter on Jacob Boehme, and you can discover how helpless a person writing an intellectual philosophy is, confronted with a spirit like Jacob Boehme.† Fortunately he left out Paracelsus, otherwise he would have written quite terrible things about him. But read what Schwegler wrote about Boehme. He found in Boehme a mind in which not the picture of ancient Saturn but a repetition of the Saturn picture had dawned in a naive way. This repetition of the Saturn picture is something that is repeated in the Earth period. In Boehme, Schwegler came upon a spirit who could do no more than try to describe with words and pictures something that could not be understood through the intellect. Every purely intellectual means of grasping the repetition of the

Saturn picture fails. It is not as if a person cannot understand these things at all, but one cannot grasp them if one only maintains the standpoint of ordinary, dry, philosophic reasoning.

You see, the important point is to lift ourselves beyond the sufficiency of ordinary intellect. Something as excellent as Schwegler's *History of Philosophy* is still produced by means of ordinary intellectual capacities and thus remains an example of how an extraordinary intellect is absolutely brought to a standstill by a spirit like Jacob Boehme.

Today, in our consideration of ancient Saturn, we have tried to penetrate the inner aspect of this ancient planetary embodiment of our Earth. In the lectures to come we will do the same with Sun and Moon existences in order to arrive at concepts that will be no less impressive than those we achieved when we looked back to ancient Saturn and allowed an imagination to arise in us of the Thrones as they sacrificed themselves to the Cherubim and thereby created the beings of time. For time is the result of sacrifice and consists of living Time. We shall see how all of these things will be transformed during the Sun existence and how other mighty processes in cosmic existence occur as we move from Saturn existence to Sun existence and then to Moon existence.

2

THE INNER ASPECT OF THE SUN EMBODIMENT OF THE EARTH

BERLIN, NOVEMBER 7, 1911

You will have gathered from the previous lecture that to describe each of the three stages of development preceding the creation of our own Earth is extremely difficult. We have seen that to do so we must first build up the concepts and ideas needed to reach such strange and distant states of our cosmic development. I have already pointed out that no description of the ancient Saturn period and the planetary embodiments of our Earth following it—such as, for example, the description given in *An Outline of Esoteric Science*—is exhaustive. In that book I had to be content to clothe the subject in pictures drawn from what is familiar and close at hand, for the book was meant to be accessible to the public and not too shocking. The description given in *An Outline of Esoteric Science* is not exactly inaccurate, but, pictorially, it is dipped in illusion or maya. One must work through the illusion to penetrate to the truth.

For example, ancient Saturn may be described as a heavenly body that did not consist of those components we know as earth, water, or air, but was made up entirely of warmth—and this is correct within certain limits. Likewise, any reference to space is only a pictorial description for, as we saw in the last lecture, not even time existed on ancient Saturn. There was no space on ancient Saturn, at least not in our sense of that term; while time first came into being then. When we put ourselves in the context of ancient Saturn, then, we are in a realm of spaceless eternity. Thus, if we attempt to picture this, we must be clear that it is only a picture.

Were we then to have entered ancient Saturn's "space," we would have found no substance there dense enough to be described as gas. There would have been only warmth and coldness. In reality, we could not speak of coming out of one part of space and entering another. There was only the feeling of moving between warmer and colder conditions. Even clairvoyants who imagine themselves within the time period of ancient Saturn experience only the impression of the ebb and flow of spaceless warmth. But this impression is only the outer veil of the Saturn state. For this warmth or fire, as we call it in esotericism, reveals itself to us in its spiritual substrata; and, as we have seen, spiritual actions, spiritual accomplishments, were in fact occurring on ancient Saturn.

We have tried to make a picture of what kind of spiritual activity was occurring on ancient Saturn. We said that the Spirits of Will, the Thrones, performed deeds of sacrifice. This means that, if we look back upon what took place on Saturn, we see the Cherubim and the sacrifice that flowed from the Thrones. Sacrifice flowed from the Thrones to the Cherubim, and these acts of sacrifice appear, when viewed from the outside, as warmth. Conditions of warmth are thus the outer, physical expression of sacrifice. Indeed, wherever we perceive warmth in the entire cosmos, this warmth is the outward expression of what stands behind it. Warmth is an illusion. Acts of sacrifice by spiritual beings are the reality behind the warmth. If we wish to characterize warmth accurately, therefore, we must say: *Cosmic warmth is the revelation of cosmic sacrifice or cosmic acts of sacrifice.*

Then we have seen, too, that as the Thrones present their sacrificial deed to the Cherubim, what we call time is simultaneously born. I have already mentioned that "time" is a modern word that does not quite fit what I am trying to describe. Time here does not yet encompass the abstractions "earlier" and "later" as we perceive them today. Time began as a configuration of spiritual beings, the Spirits of Personality also identified as "Time Spirits." These Time Spirits are really the ancient manifestation of time, the offspring of the Thrones and Cherubim. But the circumstances under which the beings of the time-aspect originated in ancient Saturn are deeds of sacrifice.

If we wish to reach a true understanding of what stands behind the warmth—when it is said that ancient Saturn consists of warmth—we must not adopt merely outwardly physical concepts. Remember that warmth as we use the term is a physical concept. Instead, we must adopt concepts derived from the life of the *soul*—the moral, wisdom-filled life of the soul. No one can know what warmth is who cannot imagine what it means to sacrifice willingly what one possesses, what one has, even what one is. One must come to understand what it means, from the perspective of the soul, to offer up one's own being, to renounce oneself consciously. In other words, one must imagine giving one's best for the healing of the world, not holding one's best for the sake of self, but wanting to sacrifice one's best at the altar of cosmic all. If we grasp all this as living concept and as a feeling permeating our soul, it can lead us gradually to understand what stands behind the appearance of warmth.

Try to imagine what is connected with the concept of sacrifice in modern life—namely, that it is inconceivable that a person who sacrifices with understanding does so against his or her will. If someone sacrifices against his or her will, the person must have felt pressed to do so. There must have been coercion. But that is not at all what is meant by sacrifice here. Here sacrifice flows as a matter of course from the being who offers it. If someone sacrifices without external coercion or the expectation of achieving something—if someone sacrifices out of an inner sense of urgency—then that person will experience inner warmth and bliss. When we feel aglow with inner warmth and happiness, this expresses something we can only describe by saying that *a person who offers a sacrifice and feels permeated with warmth glows with happiness.* We ourselves can experience how the glow of sacrifice approaches us in the illusion of external warmth in the world. Only a person who can grasp that, where there is warmth in the world there is an underlying soul-spiritual reality, truly understands what warmth is. Warmth exists and becomes active through the joy of sacrifice. Whoever can experience warmth in this way gradually arrives at the reality that exists or lies hidden behind the phenomenon, the illusion, of physical warmth.

If now we wish to press forward from ancient Saturn existence to ancient Sun existence, we must lay the basis for concepts with which to create an image of the substance of *ancient* Sun, not our present Sun. Once again, in *An Outline of Esoteric Science* I presented only the outward appearance. Ancient Sun enhanced warmth by adding air and light to it. Just as we had to search beyond warmth to perceive the glow of sacrifice brought about by the Spirits of Will, so too now—if we wish to understand the air and light that were added to warmth on ancient Sun—we must look for something *moral* as the essence of air and light. Only if we look for what we can experience within ourselves in a soul-spiritual way can we arrive at an idea, a representation, a feeling, of the air and light on ancient Sun.

We can describe this feeling as a soul experience in the following way. Imagine that you observed a genuine deed of sacrifice or imagined the Thrones presenting their sacrifice to the Cherubim, as we described it in the last lecture, and that you were so moved by this picture of sacrifice that it enlivened your soul with bliss. What would your soul feel if you were to observe such sacrificing beings or if you were to imagine a picture of this kind that awakened and enlivened your soul? If you have feelings full of life—if you cannot stand unfeelingly before the delight one feels in a deed of sacrifice—you would have to experience a profound awakening at the sight of this act of sacrifice. You would have to feel in your soul that to gaze upon the supreme happiness that arises from sacrifice is the most beautiful deed, the most beautiful experience that could ever arise in the soul!

Another feeling that would arise is an attitude of complete surrender. Indeed, you would have to be a block of wood if sacrifice did not create a longing in the soul to gaze upon it with absolute devotion and convey a mood of self-surrender. Consider such selfless giving over of oneself! A deed of sacrifice is active. It is self-surrender transformed in activity. And contemplation of active, concerned self-surrender can create an affinity for the giving over of oneself, for losing oneself—for forgetting about self. If we cannot create such a mood, or at least an inkling or an echo of it, we can never truly come to a closer understanding of sacrifice.

Indeed, if we pour this mood of disinterested giving up of self into the soul, we may reach what a higher form of knowledge can give us. A person who is unable to create a spirit of self-surrender cannot achieve higher knowledge. What is the opposite of this attitude of self-surrender? It is self-will, the assertion of one's own will. These are two poles in the soul's life: loss of self in what one is contemplating and self-willed assertion of what lies within the self. These are two great opposites. If you wish to attain real knowledge and permeate yourself with wisdom, self-will is lethal. In ordinary life, we know self-will only as prejudice—and prejudices always destroy higher insight.

In fact, one must intensify in one's thinking what I am describing here as capacity for self-surrender, for only through an intensified sense of self-surrender can a human being work toward the higher worlds. In the higher worlds, one must be able to experience the capacity to lose oneself—at least as a mood of soul. Let me emphasize here that we can never attain higher knowledge if we work only with ordinary scientific knowledge or everyday thinking. We must be clear that ordinary science and everyday thinking work out of ordinary human will, through all that self-will has created in the experiences, feelings, and ideas we have inherited or cultivated. We can be misled here—indeed, delusions are very common in this area. People come, for example, and say: We are supposed to accept this or that aspect of knowledge presented by spiritual science, but I will not accept anything that is not consistent with what I already think: I won't accept anything without proof. Certainly, one should accept nothing without evidence. But if we take from what is presented to us only what we already know, we cannot advance a step! Those who wish to become clairvoyant will never say that they will accept only what they have already proved. They must also be absolutely free from all self-seeking and know in advance that all that comes to them from the cosmos can only be described by the word *grace*. Such people anticipate everything and anything from illuminating grace. For how does one achieve clairvoyant knowledge? Only by setting aside everything we have already learned. Ordinarily, we think: I have my own judgment. But we must remember that ordinary judgment only comes out of renewing what your ancestors once thought, or what stimulates your desires, and so on. It is never a question of making one's own judgments. Those who most insist that they are exercising their own judgment are the least aware how slavishly they are tied to their own prejudices. All of this must be eliminated if we wish to attain higher knowledge. The soul must be empty and quietly able to wait for what it can receive out of the spaceless, timeless, objectless, eventless, secret, hidden world. On no account should we believe that we can acquire higher knowledge unless we allow to ripen within us a mood out of which we meet all that is offered to us as revelation or enlightenment-illumination. Only in this mood can we await whatever approaches us and gives us something as nothing other than grace, as what *should* come to us.

How does such knowledge reveal itself? How is what comes to us revealed when we have sufficiently prepared ourselves? It reveals itself as a feeling of being blessed by a gift from the spiritual world that comes to meet us. If we wished to describe what stands before us in life in this way, full of blessing and filling us with this recognition—be it a being or anything else—we could express it only as follows. We experience what comes to us as bestowing a blessing, as granting a gift, as giving us something. To grasp the nature of a being, whose main characteristic consists of the capacity for granting, giving, offering—for showering and pouring forth blessings—to grasp such a nature we would need to grasp the image of the sacrifice of the Thrones to the Cherubim! Imagine that a being came to someone who understood the meaning of the Thrones' sacrifice to the Cherubim—a being who would transform the capacity to understand the Thrones' sacrifice into a capacity to give—to pour one's gifts around oneself in blessing. Imagine that we are looking at a rose and are delighted by it, thus experiencing the feeling of being blessed by something we see as "beautiful." Then imagine another being who, by comprehending the significance of the Thrones' sacrifice to the Cherubim, could confer all that it had on its surroundings, pouring everything available into the world, in the spirit of giving—if we imagine such beings, then we have those Spirits of Wisdom described in *An Outline of Esoteric Science* who, during Sun existence, were added to those we came to know during Saturn existence.

Now, if I were to ask what is the character of these Spirits of Wisdom who appeared during Sun existence and were added to the spirits already present during the Saturn existence, I would have to answer as follows. These spirits have as their defining characteristic the virtue of giving, of bestowing, of effecting blessings. If I wanted to find a designation for these beings, I would have to say: They are the Spirits of Wisdom, the mighty Grantors, the great Givers of the Cosmos! Just as we have called the Thrones the great Sacrificers, so we have to say of the Spirits of Wisdom that they are the great Givers, who grant their gift which is the same gift as that out of which the cosmos is woven and lives, for they themselves streamed out into the cosmos and first created order.

That is the effect of the Spirits of Wisdom on the Sun: they give their own beings into their surroundings. But what, we may ask, happens on the Sun, if we want to see with higher sense perception what is represented to outer observation?

When we look at the Sun, we observe what is described in *An Outline of Esoteric Science*. In addition to warmth, the Sun also consists of air and light. But to say simply that the Sun consists of air and light as well as of warmth is the same as saying, for example, of landscape: In the distance I see a gray cloud. If one were a painter and had this impression, one would paint a gray cloud. But if one were to approach it more closely, one would perhaps find something like a swarm of insects rather than a gray cloud. Actually, what seemed like a gray cloud was a number of living beings. We are in a similar situation when we consider ancient Sun existence from a distance. From afar, ancient Sun appears to be a body consisting of air and light. But, if we look at it more closely, we no longer see a body of air and light. Instead, there appears the great virtue of bestowing by the Spirits of Wisdom. No one discovers the true nature of air who merely describes air according to outward, physical properties. These properties are only illusion (maya), external manifestations. Wherever there is air in the universe, the actions of the gift-granting Spirits of

Wisdom lie behind it. Weaving, working air reveals the virtue of bestowing by the Spirits of the Macrocosm. Only the person who sees the true nature of air, says: I perceive here the element of air, but, in reality, the Spirits of Wisdom are placing their gifts into their surroundings; something streams into the environment from the Spirits of Wisdom.

Thus we know now what we have really said about ancient Sun when we say that it consists of air. We know now that what appears outwardly as air is actually the activity of the Spirits of Wisdom allowing their own being to flow forth into their surroundings. But at this point something remarkable presents itself to clairvoyant vision on the ancient Sun. To understand this we must become clear how, out of the life of the soul, we can create an even more accurate idea of the virtue of bestowing. Let us recreate a feeling such as we can have when we are able to permeate ourselves with a perception or an idea in the mood of sacrifice that we have described here. An idea so permeated always gives us a particular feeling. It is not like a scientific idea. The most similar experience may be found in the artistic realm where, in order to give the world an independent entity, an idea must master the way in which color or form streams out into the world.

To characterize a being who has the capacity to give such a gift, one may say that productivity, creativity is bound up with this gift, for the act itself of giving is a creative activity. Whoever has an idea and feels that the idea can bring healing into the world, and then presents it in works of art, has rightly understood the fruits of the virtue of bestowing. Think of a creative idea in the mind of the artist, and how it then becomes manifest in matter: this idea is actually a spiritual being of air. 'Where air exists, we face creative activity. And because this living creativity existed on the Sun, the association of air with creative ability is identifiable as fact.

If we recall that the Spirits of Time were born on ancient Saturn, we also know that time existed on the Sun—for time came over to the Sun from Saturn. Time existed there. Because the archetypal bestowing arose, a possibility existed on ancient Sun that could not have occurred on ancient Saturn. Consider what would have become of giving if time had not existed: there would be no bestowing, for giving consists both of giving and receiving. Without receiving, giving is inconceivable. Thus giving consists of two acts: giving and receiving. Otherwise giving has no purpose. On the Sun, giving stands in a most unusual relation to receiving. Because time already exists on the Sun, the gift, sent into the surroundings of the ancient Sun, is preserved in time. When the Spirits of Wisdom pour out their gifts, they remain present in time. Something must then enter that is capable of receiving. In relationship to the activity of the Spirits of Wisdom receiving occurs at a later point in time. The Spirits of Wisdom give at an earlier moment, and what is necessarily bound up with their giving as receiving occurs at a later point in time.

To gain an accurate picture of this, once again we must take the experience of our own soul into account. Imagine that you have tried very hard to understand something or to formulate some thought. Now you have created this thought. The next day you clear your mind, so that everything that you created in your thoughts on the previous day can be brought back to mind. Thus, you receive today what was formulated yesterday. So it was on the ancient Sun: what was given at an earlier point in time remained preserved and then was received at a later moment. But what was the significance of this receiving?

Like the archetypal giving, receiving, too, is a deed or event on the ancient Sun. Receiving differentiates itself from giving only in terms of time. Receiving occurs later. The giving comes from the Spirits of Wisdom. But who receives? Before someone can receive, there first must be a recipient. In the same way that the sacrifice of the Thrones to the Cherubim brought about the birth of the Spirits of Time on Saturn, the birth of bestowing in the universe by the Spirits of Wisdom on the Sun created those spirits we call Archangels or Archangeloi. The Archangels are the ones who receive on the ancient Sun. But they receive in a very special manner, for what the Archangels receive from the Spirits of Wisdom, they do not keep for themselves. Rather they reflect it back, just as a mirror reflects back the image it receives. Thus the Archangels on the Sun have the task of receiving what was given at an earlier point in time, so that it is preserved and reflected again by the Archangels into a later time. Therefore, on the Sun, we have an earlier act of giving and a later act of receiving, but a receiving in the form of a streaming or reflecting back of what was given at the earlier point in time.

Imagine that the earth were not as it currently is, but that what had happened during an earlier time could stream once again into the present. We know that something like that actually occurs. We live in the fifth post-Atlantean cultural epoch and the events of the third post-Atlantean cultural period, the ancient Egypto-Chaldean era, stream into this period. What occurred during the third epoch will reemerge and be reflected back again. That is a recapitulation of the giving and receiving that occurred during the ancient Sun development. Thus we may think of the Spirits of Wisdom as the bestowers in ancient Sun times and the Archangels as the receivers. Something quite remarkable arises from this, which you can represent accurately only by imagining an inwardly enclosed globe from whose center radiates something to be given away. Something radiates out from the center to the periphery and from there reflects back to the middle point. From within the outer surface of the globe the Archangels radiate back what they have received. From the outside you need not imagine anything. We must imagine something moving out from the center that comes from the Spirits of Wisdom. It radiates in all directions and is received by the Archangels who reflect it back again. 'What is it that reflects back into space? 'What is this gift of the Spirits of Wisdom that radiates back again? What is the radiating wisdom that is directed back to its source? It is *light*. The Archangels are also the creators of light. Light is not at all what it appears to be in outward illusion. Where light occurs, the gifts of the Spirits of Wisdom are radiating back to us. And the beings whose existence we must presume wherever there is light are the Archangels. Thus we must say: the Archangels are hidden within the flooding rays of light. Behind the flooding rays of light that come to us the Archangels are hidden. The Archangels' capacity to stream forth light arises out of the virtue of bestowing that is radiated to them by the Spirits of Wisdom.

We thus arrive at a picture of the old Sun. Imagine a center where the Spirits of Wisdom are immersed in their contemplation of the legacy from ancient Saturn—the deed of sacrifice of the Thrones to the Cherubim. Contemplating this deed of sacrifice causes the

Spirits of Wisdom to radiate the substance of their own being—to radiate streaming, flowing wisdom in the form of the virtue of bestowing. Because this virtue is permeated by time, it is sent forth and then reflected back again, so that we have before us a globe, illumined *within* by virtue reflected back to its source and center. For we must imagine that the ancient Sun illuminates in an inward, not an outward direction. And this creates something new that we can describe in the following way. Imagine these Spirits of Wisdom, seated at the center of the Sun, contemplating the sacrificing Thrones and radiating their own being far out into their surroundings. Then, from the surface of the globe, they receive back what they radiated forth in the form of light. Everything is illuminated through and through. But what do they receive from what radiates back to them? Their own being, their innermost being, has been surrendered as a gift to the macrocosm. Now it radiates back—their own being returns to them from the outside. They see their own inner being distributed throughout the cosmos and radiated back as light, as the reflection of their own being.

Inner and outer are the two opposites that now come before us. The earlier and the later transform themselves and become the inner and the outer. Space is born! Out of the gift of the virtue of bestowing given by the Spirits of Wisdom space arises on the old Sun. Before this, space could have only allegorical meaning. Now, however, on the old Sun, we actually have space, but only in two dimensions: there are no above and below, no right and left, only outer and inner. Actually these two opposites already emerge at the end of ancient Saturn, but they recapitulate the process in the creation of space on ancient Sun.

And if we want to imagine all of these occurrences again—just as previously we brought before our soul the sacrificing Thrones giving birth to the Time Spirits—we would not portray a body consisting of light, for light does not yet radiate outward but exists only as reflection radiating inward. Rather, we must imagine a globe as inner space. At its center, a recapitulation of the picture of Saturn occurs: the Thrones present as spirits kneeling before the Cherubim—those winged beings who offer their own being—and, in addition to these, the Spirits of Wisdom immersed in contemplation of the sacrifice. Now one can imagine that the glow lying within the sacrifice (the sacrificial fire of the Thrones), transforms itself into the sacrifice of the Spirits of Wisdom: their sacrifice is represented materially as air that rises during the act of sacrifice as sacrificial smoke. Thus we have a complete picture if we imagine:

- the sacrificing Thrones kneeling before the Cherubim,
- the choirs of Spirits of Wisdom surrendering in devotion to the vision of the sacrifice of the Thrones at the center of the Sun,
- their devotion growing into an image of sacrificial smoke, which spreads out in all directions, streams outward, condenses into clouds at the periphery,
- the Archangels being created out of the clouds of smoke,
- the gift of the sacrificial smoke radiating back from the periphery in the form of light,
- the light illuminating the interior of the Sun,
- the gift of the Spirits of Wisdom being given back, thereby creating the sphere of the Sun.

This sphere consists of the outpoured gifts of glowing warmth and sacrificial smoke. At the outer periphery sit the Archangels, the creators of light, who reflect what earlier came into being on the Sun. It took time, but eventually sacrificial smoke could return as light. What were the Archangels preserving? They preserved what arose earlier, the gifts of the Spirits of Wisdom that the Archangels received and then radiated back. But what previously existed as time they gave back as space, and, by radiating back time as space, the Archangels gave back what they themselves had received from the Archai. Thus they become the Angels of Beginning, because they brought what existed earlier into a later time. Archangels—Messengers of Beginning!†

It is remarkable when, out of true esoteric knowledge, a "Word" such as this re-emerges, and when we recall how this "Word," arising in the most ancient traditions, has been passed on to us through the school of Dionysius the Areopagite,† the pupil of Paul. It is remarkable to see that this word is so deeply imprinted that, when we discover it again, independently of what was written, what originally arose—the original meaning—arises again. That fills us with the greatest respect. We feel linked to the ancient, holy Mystery schools of initiation wisdom. It is as if this ancient tradition were streaming into us, for we grasp it with understanding, even though we ourselves are responsible for acquiring this knowledge independently of the old tradition. Those who can experience something of the mood of the ancient forms of expression that have been handed down to us, even though they may be unaware of these traditions, feel themselves placed under the influence of the Time Spirits within the human spirit. A wonderful feeling of being linked with the whole of human evolution arises from this: a feeling of certainty in these matters.

The Archangels preserve the recollection of the archetypal beginnings. Whatever existed on one or another of the planets is recapitulated at a later time, but something else is always added to the later manifestation. Thus, in a certain way, we also meet the Being of the Sun in what we find on our own Earth.

This entire imagination, this whole feeling that we can develop, gives us an image of the sacrificing Thrones, of the Cherubim receiving their offering, of the glow radiating from the sacrifice, of the sacrificial smoke spreading out like air, of the light radiating back from the Archangels who preserve what occurred in the beginning for a later time. This feeling can awaken in us an understanding of everything related to these creations.

This milieu, which I have portrayed here as a milieu of the soul, presents from a more spiritual perspective what we earlier attained through a physical representation. And we shall now see that it is out of this milieu that the being is born who appeared on the Earth as the Christ Being. We can understand what the Christ Being brought to the Earth only if we assimilate the concept of the grace-engendering virtue of bestowing as it reflects in the light of the cosmos into the inner substance of the Sun body—which is permeated and illuminated by this light. If we hold up this image, which we have just described, transform it into an imagination and consider that this is what this being brought to and embodied on Earth, then we will be able to experience more deeply the spiritual being of the Christ impulse. We will be able to understand the dim inkling that can live in the human soul when it senses that what has just been described by this representation can live again on Earth.

Let us imagine that what we have just described of the Sun was gathered up and concentrated completely in the soul of a being and then, at a later time, brought forward again. Imagine that this being appeared on Earth and worked in such a way that out of what the archetypal deed and smoke of sacrifice created—that is, the light-engendering time and the bestowing virtue—an extract of activating grace would be carried over and reflect soul warmth and glorious light out of the cosmos. Imagine all of this concentrated in a single soul, who in turn gives this to the Earth existence, and that assembled around this soul are those who are intended to radiate this back and preserve it for the remainder of the Earth existence. In the center is the one who bestows out of the sacrifice and through sacrifice; around this being are those who are intended to receive it. Here we have linked together, on the one hand, what the sacrifice is and what belongs to it, translated into earthly existence, and, on the other hand, the possibility of destroying this sacrifice, for everything that can be given to the human being to bring about grace may be either rejected or accepted. Imagine that all of this were embodied in an intuition—then one would have what one experiences standing before Leonardo da Vinci's *Last Supper*: here we have the entire Sun together with the beings of sacrifice, the beings of bestowing virtue, the beings of soul-warming bliss and light-filled splendor—as grasped by the soul—radiated back from the ones who have been chosen to preserve what arises in earlier times for later times. All this has been set out especially for the Earth, together with the possibility that it can also be rejected by the betrayer.

The Being of the Earth, insofar as the Being of the Sun reappears on the Earth, can be experienced in this way. If this is felt not in an outward, intellectual manner, but in a truly artistic way, one can experience the real driving force in such a great work of art that reflects an extract of Earth existence. And if next time we see this picture we notice how the Christ grows out of the Sun milieu, then we will understand more fully what we have often said: that if a spirit came down from Mars to the Earth and could not understand everything he saw, that spirit would still be able to understand the mission of the Earth if he allowed Leonardo's *Last Supper* to work upon him. An inhabitant of Mars would be able to see that Sun existence must be concealed within Earth existence, and everything that we could say about the significance of this for the Earth would be clear to him. That inhabitant of Mars would understand that the Earth has meaning, and know what was significant for the Earth. He would say to himself: "This could occur somewhere on Earth and have meaning only for a corner of the Earth's existence. But if this deed could really be represented, the deed that streams toward me out of the colors of the central figure in relation to the surrounding figures, then I would feel what the Spirits of Wisdom experienced on the Sun echoing again here in the words: Do this in remembrance of me! Here is the preservation of the earlier in the later. We will only understand these words when we grasp them in the context of the entire cosmos, as we have just learned to do. Here I just wanted to point out how an artistic deed of the first rank stands in relationship to the entire development of the cosmos.

In the next lecture it will be our task to understand the Christ Being from the perspective of the Spiritual Being of the Sun in order to go on to the perspective of the Spiritual Being of the Moon.

3

THE INNER ASPECT OF THE SUN EMBODIMENT OF THE EARTH AND THE TRANSITION TO THE MOON EMBODIMENT

BERLIN, NOVEMBER 14, 1911

In the last two lectures I tried to point out that something spiritual lies behind all that is material in the phenomena in our universe. I tried to characterize the spiritual reality to be found behind the phenomena of warmth and streaming air. To describe such characteristics for you, I had to reach back into the most distant past of our evolutionary development. We also looked into our own soul life to describe the spiritual context that forms the basis of the material universe. After all, when we characterize something we must take the ideas we use from somewhere else. Words alone are not enough: one must have very definite ideas.

We have seen that the spiritual context which we must refer to lies far from anything human beings experience at the present time, far from what human beings today are able to know. Thus, to understand this context, we have to call upon conditions seldom found and contexts not generally understood in our own life of soul and spirit. We have seen that we have had to search for the deepest nature of the conditions of warmth and fire far from the manifestation of outward, physical fire or warmth. Certainly, when we identify sacrifice—indeed, the sacrifice of specific beings, the Thrones, whom we met during the ancient Saturn state of the Earth's development, and who at that time presented their sacrifice to the Cherubim—as the essence of all conditions of fire and warmth in the cosmos, this must seem fantastic to a person today. And yet, to speak truly, we must say that as it occurred at that point in the development of the cosmos, everything that appears to us outwardly, illusorily, in the condition of warmth or fire actually consists of sacrifice.

Similarly, we pointed out last time that behind everything that we call streaming air or gas lies something very distant—namely, what we have called the virtue of bestowing, the devoted pouring forth of their own being by spiritual beings. That is what exists in every breath of wind, in every stream of air. What is perceived as outwardly physical is really only an illusion, maya. Only when we have progressed from the illusion to the spiritual reality, will we have a correct idea. Fire or warmth or air are no more present as realities in the world than the human being is present in the image a person sees in a mirror. For, as a mirror image is essentially an illusion in relation to the human being, so fire or warmth or air are illusions, and the truths behind them are the reality—just as the real human being stands in relation to his or her image in the mirror. It is not fire or air that we seek in the realm of the true, but sacrifice and the virtue of bestowing.

When we saw the virtue of bestowing added to sacrifice, we ascended from the ancient life of Saturn to that of the Sun. Within the second embodiment of our Earth, we find something that leads us a step nearer to the true circumstances of our development. And here we must once again introduce a concept that belongs to the realm of true reality as opposed to the world of illusion. That is, before we take up the actual circumstances of our evolutionary development, we must acquire a particular concept.

Let us approach this concept as follows. When a human being in his or her outward life does something or accomplishes something, this generally results from his or her will impulse. Whatever a human being does, whether it is just a hand movement or a mighty deed, a will impulse stands behind the activity. Everything that leads a person to carry out a deed or to achieve something emanates from this. And it will probably be said that a strong, forceful deed, for example, one that brings healing and blessing, proceeds from a strong will impulse, and a less important act proceeds from a weaker impulse. In general, we are inclined to assume that the magnitude of the deed depends on the strength of the impulse of will.

Only to a certain degree, however, is it correct to say that if we strengthen our will, we shall accomplish something significant in the world. Beyond a certain point, that is no longer the case. Surprisingly, certain deeds that a human being can carry out—above all, deeds connected with the spiritual world—are not dependent upon the strengthening of our will impulse. Of course, in the physical world in which we live, the magnitude of the deed does depend on the strength of the will impulse: we have to make a greater effort if we want to accomplish more. But in the spiritual world this is not the case, rather the opposite applies. To accomplish the greatest deeds, to achieve the greatest results in the spiritual world, a strengthening of the positive will impulse is not what is necessary, rather a certain resignation, a renunciation is needed. We can proceed on that assumption even in the smallest, purely spiritual matters. We achieve a certain spiritual result not by bringing our earnest desires into play or being occupied with them, but by subduing our wishes, restraining our desires, and forgoing their satisfaction.

Let us suppose that a person intended to accomplish something in the world through inner spiritual means. The individual has to prepare himself or herself by learning above all to suppress his or her wishes or desires. And while one becomes stronger in the physical world if one eats well and is well nourished and thus has more energy, one will achieve something significant in the spiritual world—this is a description, not advice—when one fasts or does something to suppress or renounce wishes and desires. Preparation that involves relinquishing the wishes, desires, and will impulses arising in us is always part of the greatest spiritual endeavors. The less we will, the more we can say that we let life stream over us and do not desire this or that, but rather take things as karma casts them before us; the more we accept karma and its consequences; the more we behave calmly, renouncing all that we otherwise would have wanted to achieve in life—the stronger we become. This is true, for example, in respect to the activity of thinking.

In the instance of a teacher or educator who is filled with longings and above all is fond of good food and drink, it will become evident that the words he or she directs at pupils do not accomplish very much: what the teacher says to the students goes right in one ear and out the other. Such a teacher will believe that the students are to blame for this, but that is not always the case. An educator who sees a higher meaning in life, lives in moderation, eats only as much as is necessary in order to sustain life, and above all accepts by choice the things that destiny bestows, will gradually notice that his or her words have great power. Even the glance of such a teacher can have a great effect. Indeed, it may not even be necessary for the teacher to look at a pupil. Such a teacher need only be near the student, need only have an encouraging thought. Even if the thought is not expressed verbally, it is nonetheless conveyed to the student. All of this depends upon the degree of renunciation and resignation a person exercises with regard to what is otherwise strongly desired.

The path of renunciation is the right means of spiritual activity and leads to spiritual results in higher worlds. In this respect we can encounter many illusions—and even though an illusion of renunciation seems outwardly similar to true renunciation, illusions do not lead to the right results. You are all acquainted with what is called, in ordinary life, asceticism: self-inflicted suffering. In many cases such self-torment can be self-indulgence, something a person chooses from a desire to accomplish something greater or out of some other source of desire for self-satisfaction. In such cases, self-denial is not effective, for self-denial has meaning only when it accompanies renunciation that is rooted in the spirit. We must understand the concept of creative renunciation, creative resignation. It is extremely important that we recognize renunciation or creative resignation—which we can actually experience in the soul—as an idea that is far removed from everyday life. Only then will we be able to take a step further in human evolution. For something like this occurred in the course of evolution in the transition from the development of the Sun condition to that of the Moon condition. Something like resignation occurred then in the realm of the beings of the higher worlds who, as we know, are linked to the course of the Earth's development. To understand this we shall need to consider the ancient Sun development once again. But, first, we will draw attention to something we already know, but which may have seemed puzzling in some respects up until now.

We have pointed repeatedly to precedents in development that we can trace back to beings who remained behind in the course of development.† We know, indeed, that luciferic beings intrude upon humankind on earth. And we have frequently pointed out that these luciferic beings, because they did not reach the stage of development that they could have achieved during the development of the ancient Moon, are able to invade our astral body during earthly evolution. In this context, we have often used the trivial comparison that it is not only students who repeat a grade at school, but cosmic beings in the great course of cosmic evolution may also fail to complete a stage of development and later interfere in the stages of development of other beings. Thus luciferic beings, who stayed behind during the ancient Moon development, interfere with human beings on the Earth.

Superficially, one could easily think that these beings must be flawed beings, weaklings in world evolution—otherwise why did they fail to achieve what they could have achieved? That thought could occur to us. But another thought we could also formulate is that human beings would never have come into their freedom, would never have developed an independent capacity to make decisions, had luciferic beings not been held back on the Moon. On the one hand, it is due to luciferic beings that we have desires, drives, and passions in our astral body that continually drive us from a certain height and pull us toward the lower regions of our being. On the other hand, however, were it not for our capacity to become evil and stray from the good through the power of the luciferic beings in our astral body, we could not act freely or have what we call free will or freedom of choice. It must be said, therefore, that we owe our freedom to the luciferic beings. The one-sided perspective that luciferic beings exist only to lead humanity astray is insufficient. Rather, we must regard the remaining behind of the luciferic beings as something good, and as something without which we would not be able to achieve our worth as human beings in the true sense of the word.

Yet something much deeper lies at the basis of what we call the remaining behind of the luciferic and ahrimanic beings. We have already encountered it on ancient Saturn, but it is so difficult to recognize that we can hardly find words in any language to characterize it. Yet, we can characterize it very clearly if we move forward to the reality of the ancient Sun by taking into account the concept of resignation or renunciation we described today. For the basis of the remaining behind of beings and the influence stemming from it lies in resignation or renunciation on the part of higher beings.

We can see, then, that the following occurred on the Sun. We have said that the Thrones—the Spirits of Will—offer sacrifice to the Cherubim. They present this sacrifice, as we saw last time, not only during the Saturn era; they continue to do so during the Sun era. The Thrones, the Spirits of Will, sacrifice to the Cherubim in the Sun era also. We saw, too, that the real essence of all that existed in the world as conditions of warmth or fire lies in this sacrifice. Now, if we look back into the Akashic record, we can notice something else occurring during the Sun period. The Thrones sacrifice, and maintain their activity of sacrifice. We see the sacrificing Thrones. We also see a number of Cherubim—to whom the sacrifice ascends—receiving the warmth that flows from the sacrifice into themselves. But at the same time a number of Cherubim do something else: they renounce the sacrifice; they do not participate in it. Recognizing this, we complete the image that we allowed to enter our soul the last time.

In this picture, we have the Thrones who sacrifice and those Cherubim who accept the sacrifice; and we also have the Cherubim who do not accept the sacrifice but give back what presses toward them as sacrifice. It is extraordinarily interesting to trace this in the Akashic Chronicle. For, because the virtue of bestowing flows from the Spirits of Wisdom into the sacrificial warmth, we see how during the ancient Sun the smoke of sacrifice, which is reflected back in the form of light by the Archangels from the outermost periphery of the Sun, ascends. But we see something else as well. It is as if, within the expanse of the ancient Sun, something entirely different is also present, namely, sacrificial smoke that is neither reflected by the Archangels as light nor accepted by the Cherubim and therefore flows back—so that we have clouds of sacrifice in the Sun expanse: sacrifice which ascends and sacrifice that descends; sacrifice that is accepted and sacrifice that is renounced and returned. We also find this self-encountering of the actual spiritual cloud image in the expanse of ancient Sun between what we called last time the outer and the inner. We find it as a separate layer between these two dimensions on the Sun. Thus, in the middle, we have the sacrificing Thrones, in the heights the Cherubim who accept the sacrifice, and then those Cherubim who do not accept the sacrifice but divert it back again. Through this "diverting back" a ring of clouds comes into being, and around this we have the reflected mass of light.

Imagine this picture in a living way. We have this ancient Sun expanse, this ancient Sun mass, like a cosmic globe, beyond which nothing is imaginable, so that we think of space extending only as far as the Archangels. Imagine that at the center we have a ring formation made out of the meeting between the accepted and rejected sacrifices. Out of these accepted and returned sacrifices arises something in the ancient Sun that we can call a division of the entire Sun substance, a divergence. If we wish to compare the ancient Sun to an outward image, we can compare it only to our present Saturn: a globe surrounded by a ring. The accumulating mass of the sacrifice is drawn inward into the center, and what remains outside is ordered into the form of a ring. Thus, we have the Sun substance divided into two parts, separated through the force of the arrested powers of sacrifice.

What do the Cherubim who renounce the sacrifice bring about? Here we approach an extraordinarily difficult subject. You will be able to grasp the concepts we will now consider only after a long process of meditation. Only after long reflection on the concepts to be given here will you discover the realities underlying them. The resignation we spoke of must be brought into relationship with the creation of time we learned occurred on ancient Saturn. We have seen that time first arose on ancient Saturn with the Spirits of Time, the Archai, and that it makes no sense to speak of time before ancient Saturn. Now a recapitulation occurs within this process, but, even so, it is still possible to say that time continues from that point on. Continuation, duration is a concept encompassed by the term "time." When we say, "Time is continuous," this means that when we investigate what is said about Saturn and Sun in the Akashic Chronicle, we discover that time is created during the Saturn epoch and is also present on the Sun. Now if all conditions continue in the way we characterized them with regard to Saturn and the Sun in the last two lectures, then Time would form an element in everything that happened in the course of evolution. We could not eliminate the element of time from any event in evolution. We have seen that the Spirits of Time were created on ancient Saturn, and that time is implanted in everything. And everything we have pictured or imagined about evolution since then must be conceived in the context of time. If what occurred consisted only of what we have presented—offering sacrifice and the virtue of bestowing—all of this would then have to be subject to time. Nothing would exist without being subject to time. Everything that comes into being and everything that passes away—and therefore pertains to time—everything would be subject to time.

Those Cherubim who renounced the sacrifice and at the same time what existed in the sacrificial smoke, renounced these things because they thereby deprived themselves of the properties of this sacrificial smoke. Now, among the properties of the sacrificial smoke was, above all, time, and with it, the processes of coming into being and passing away. In the whole renunciation of the sacrifice, therefore, lies a capacity of the Cherubim to grow beyond the conditions of time. These Cherubim move beyond time—they are no longer subject to time. Thus the conditions of ancient Sun's development are divided so that certain conditions, continuing in a direct line from Saturn as sacrifice and the virtue of bestowing, remain subject to time; whereas other conditions, under the direction of the Cherubim who renounced the sacrifice, wrest themselves out of time so that eternity, permanence, not being subject to the processes of coming into being and passing away may also exist. This is most remarkable: we come to the point in the development of the ancient Sun when time and eternity become separated. By means of the resignation of the Cherubim during the Sun development, eternity came about as a consequence of certain conditions that occurred during that development.

Just as, gazing into our own soul, we saw certain effects arising in the soul as the human being takes up renunciation and resignation, so we now see also eternity and immortality occur on ancient Sun because certain divine-spiritual beings have renounced sacrifice and the legacy of the virtue of bestowing. Just as we saw that time came into being on Saturn, so we see now that through certain circumstances time was wrested out of the Sun phase of development. I have said—of course, please note this—that this was already being prepared during the Saturn epoch, so that eternity does not actually begin during the Sun period. But it is only in the Sun epoch that this can be seen clearly enough to express it in concepts. The separation of eternity from time is so barely perceptible on Saturn that our concepts and words are not precise enough to characterize how something like this existed for ancient Saturn and its development.

We have now become acquainted with the meaning both of resignation—the renunciation of the gods during the time of the ancient Sun—and of the achievement of immortality. What were the further consequences of this?

From *An Outline of Esoteric Science* (although the description remains in a certain respect veiled in maya) we know that the Moon period of development followed the Sun period—that at the end of the Sun period, all existing conditions were immersed in a kind of twilight, a cosmic chaos, and that these then emerged again as Moon. We can see the emergence of sacrifice as warmth again. But what remains as warmth on the Sun emerges on the Moon as heat. What was previously the virtue of bestowing reappears as gas or air. Resignation, the renunciation of the sacrifice, also continues. What we called resignation is present in everything that occurs on the ancient Moon. This is really so: what we were able to experience as resignation on the Sun we must also think of as a force in all that exists on ancient Moon, having come over from the Sun, and as something different from what we think of as existing in the external world. What existed as sacrifice appears in maya as warmth; what was the virtue of bestowing appears as gas or air; what existed as resignation appears as liquid, as water. Outwardly, water is maya, and it would not exist in the world were it not for its spiritual foundation in renunciation or resignation. Wherever there is water in the world, there is divine renunciation!

Just as warmth is an illusion, and behind it exists sacrifice; just as gas or air is an illusion behind which stands the virtue of bestowing; so water as substance, as external reality, is only a material illusion, a reflection of what truly exists: the resignation by certain beings of what they could have received from other beings. One could say, it is only possible for water to flow in the world when resignation underlies the phenomenon. Now, we know that, during the transition from the Sun to the Moon, conditions of air densified into conditions of water. Water first came into being on the Moon; during the Sun period, there was no water. What we saw during the ancient Sun development in the gathering mass of clouds became water as it pressed together, and emerged as the Moon's ocean during the Moon period.

When we take this into account, it is possible to understand a question that can now be raised. Water arises out of resignation; in fact, water actually is resignation. Thus, we acquire a very unusual type of spiritual concept for what water really is. But we can also ask the question: Is there not a difference between the condition that would have arisen had the Cherubim not accomplished this resignation and the condition that arose when they deprived themselves of what was offered? Isn't this difference expressed in some way? Yes, it is expressed. It is expressed by the fact that the consequences of that resignation arose during the Moon conditions.

If this resignation had not occurred, if the renouncing Cherubim had accepted the sacrifice brought to them, they would have had—pictorially speaking—the sacrificial smoke within their own substance: acceptance of the sacrifice would have been expressed in the sacrificial smoke. Let us assume these Cherubim would have carried out this or that action. Then that action would appear, expressed outwardly, through self-transforming clouds of air. What the Cherubim would have done by accepting the sacrificial substance would have been expressed in the outward form of air. But they rejected the substance of sacrifice and thereby withdrew from mortality and entered immortality, withdrew from the transitory and entered the enduring. The substance of the sacrifice is still there, but is, so to speak, released from the forces that would otherwise have absorbed it. The sacrificial substance no longer needs to follow the inclinations and impulses of the Cherubim, for these Cherubim have released it, have turned it back.

What happens then with this substance of sacrifice? Other beings are able to become independent. These beings are found near the Cherubim and would have been under their direction if the latter had accepted the substance of sacrifice. But the substance is no longer within these Cherubim and is independent of them. Because of this, the possibility arises for the opposite of resignation to occur: other beings draw the poured-out substance of sacrifice to themselves and become active within it. These are the beings who remained behind, and so the presence of beings who stayed behind is a consequence of the Cherubim's act of renunciation. The Cherubim themselves produced the beings who stayed behind. Thus, they created the possibility of "remaining behind." Through the Cherubim's rejection of a sacrifice, other beings who do not renounce it, but surrender to their own wishes and desires, and bring them to expression, are able to take possession of the sacrifice and its substance, and to gain the possibility of becoming independent beings alongside the other beings.

Thus, with the transition from the development of the Sun to the Moon and with the Cherubim becoming immortal, the possibility arises for other beings to separate themselves in their own substance from the continuing development of the Cherubim, indeed, to separate themselves altogether from immortal beings. We also see, by discovering the deeper reason for remaining behind, that the responsibility—if we wish to speak about the ultimate factor of causation—for holding back these beings does not rest with the beings themselves. That is the most important point that we must grasp. If the Cherubim had accepted the sacrifice, the luciferic beings could not have remained behind, for they would not have had the opportunity to become embodied in this sacrificial substance. Renunciation was the prerequisite for beings to become independent in this way. Wise cosmic guidance orders things so that the gods themselves called their opponents into being. If the gods had not deprived themselves, it would have been impossible for beings to oppose them. Or, to express it simply, we could say that the gods were able to foresee that if they continued to create only as they had done since the transition from Saturn to the Sun, then free beings who acted out of their own initiative would never come into being. The gods recognized that in order for free beings to be created, the possibility had to be given for opponents to arise against them in the cosmic all so that they could meet resistance in whatever was subject to time. They knew that if they themselves were the only ones to order everything, they would never be able to find such opposition. We can imagine the gods acknowledging that they could make it very easy for themselves if they were to accept all of the sacrifice—for then all evolution would be subject to them. But they decided not to do that. They wanted beings who were free from them, who were capable of opposing them. Therefore the gods determined not to accept all of the sacrifice in order that beings, through the gods own resignation and the fact that the others themselves accept the sacrifice—might become their opponents!

We see, therefore, that we must not look for the origin of evil in so-called evil beings—but in so-called good beings, who by their renunciation first made it possible for evil to arise through beings capable of bringing evil into the world. Now, someone could very easily object—and I ask that you allow this thought to work very precisely within your soul—someone could object: "Until now I had a much better opinion of the gods! I used to think that the gods were capable of setting the stage for human freedom without necessarily creating evil. How is it that all of these good gods were not able to bring human freedom into the world without evil?" I would like to remind you of the Spanish king who found the world terribly complicated and commented that, if God had left the creation of the world to him, he would have made it much simpler.[†] Human beings may think, in their weakness, that the world could have been made simpler, but the gods knew better, and, therefore, did not leave the creation of the world up to human beings.

From the point of view of spiritual science, we can characterize these conditions even more exactly. Let us assume that something needs a support, and someone suggests that the necessary support could be provided by erecting a column upon which the object could then be placed. The person to whom this suggestion was addressed could then say, "But there must be another way of doing this! Yes, why shouldn't it be done in another manner?" Or someone could say, when using a triangle during construction, "Why should this triangle have only three angles? Perhaps a god could have made a triangle that did not have three angles!" But it makes as much sense to say that a triangle should not have three angles as it does to say that the gods should have created freedom without the possibility of evil and suffering. Just as three corners belong to a triangle, so to freedom belongs the possibility of evil brought about through resignation on the part of spiritual beings. All that I have been speaking of belongs to the resignation of the gods. For, in order to guide evil back to the good, after they had risen to the level of immortality by renouncing the sacrifice, the gods created evolution out of immortality. They did so by means of this very resignation. The gods did not avoid evil, which alone could grant the possibility of freedom. If the gods had suppressed evil, the world would be poor and unvaried. The gods had to allow evil to come into the world for the sake of human freedom, and therefore they also had to acquire the strength necessary to lead evil back to the good. And this capacity is something that can come about only as a consequence of renunciation and resignation.

Religions always exist to portray the great cosmic mysteries in pictures and imaginations. We have referred to the ancient phases of development today, and by adding the concept of resignation to those of sacrifice and the virtue of bestowing, we have taken another step into true reality in contrast to maya and illusion. Religion gives us such pictures and concepts. Therefore in biblical religion, too, we can gain access to the concepts of sacrifice and the resignation or rejection of the sacrifice. For instance, there is the story of Abraham, who was going to present his own son as a sacrifice to God, and of God's forgoing the patriarch's sacrifice. If we take this concept of "forgoing" into our soul, then meditative images such as we have already formulated also come to us. Once I suggested that we assume the sacrifice of Abraham had been accepted and that Isaac was sacrificed.† If God had accepted this sacrifice, the entire ancient Hebrew people, who stem from Isaac, would have been taken from the earth. By renouncing the sphere of the Hebrew people, withdrawing it from his circle of influence, so that it came to be outside him, God granted as a gift all who derive from Abraham. If God had accepted Abraham's sacrifice, God would have taken into himself the whole sphere where the ancient Hebrew people were active, for the sacrificed Isaac would have been together with God. God relinquished this course, however, and thereby allowed this entire line of evolution to transpire on earth. All concepts of resignation, of sacrifice, can be awakened in us through the deeply meaningful picture of sacrifice presented by the ancient patriarch.

We can find another instance of resignation or sacrifice by higher beings in earthly history, and here, too, we may refer to something that we already mentioned last time—namely, Leonardo da Vinci's painting, *The Last Supper*. Imagine that scene in which we have before us at the same time the essential meaning of both the Earth and the Christ. Let us penetrate the full meaning of the picture, and so let us recall the words we find in the Gospel: "Could I not summon a whole choir of angels, if I wanted to avoid the sacrifice of death?"†

With resignation and renunciation Christ refused this obvious and easy solution he could have invoked. The greatest example of renunciation that Christ Jesus brings before us occurred when he allowed his betrayer, Judas Iscariot, to enter his sphere. If we are to see in Christ Jesus what we should be able to see in him, we must see in him a reflection of those beings who had to renounce sacrifice and whose very nature is that of resignation. The Christ renounced what would have occurred if he had not allowed Judas to act as his opponent, just as the gods themselves during the time of the ancient Sun called forth their own opponents through their deed of renunciation. So we see this event—the coming forth of the opponents to cosmic powers—repeated pictorially on Earth. We see Christ in the midst of the twelve, together with Judas, who stood there as the betrayer. In order that what is of incomparable worth to humankind could enter the course of development, Christ himself had to place his opponent in opposition to himself.

This picture makes a profound impression upon us, because gazing at *The Last Supper* reminds us of a powerful, cosmic moment. Holding before us the words of Christ, "He who dipped his hand with me in the dish will betray me,"† we see the earthly reflection of the opponents of the gods set in opposition to the gods by the gods themselves. I often say that everything that inhabitants of Mars would see, were they to descend to Earth, would be more or less interesting, even if they were not able to understand it fully. But by looking at this picture by Leonardo da Vinci, such Martians would discover something from a cosmic perspective that would be relevant not only to the Earth but to Mars as well and, indeed, to the entire solar system. And thereby the significance of the Earth would be recognized. What is portrayed in *The Last Supper* in an earthly picture has meaning for the whole cosmos: the setting into opposition of certain powers over against the immortal, divine powers. And Christ, who overcame death and demonstrated the triumph of immortality on Earth—and appears in the midst of his apostles—gives evidence of a significant, cosmic moment that arose as the gods differentiated themselves from time-bound beings and achieved a victory over time, that is, became immortal. All this may be felt in our hearts when we look at The Last Supper by Leonardo da Vinci.

Please do not say that one who views *The Last Supper* with simple, naive sensitivity does not understand what we have said today. Such a person does not need to know these things. For the mysterious depth of the human soul is such that one does not need to know intellectually what is felt in the human soul. Does the flower know the laws by which it grows? No, but it grows in spite of that. What need has a flower for natural law? What need then has a human soul for reason—for intellect—if we are to feel the incomparable magnitude of what is there before us, when spread out before our eyes we see a god and that god's opponent, when the loftiest that is capable of being expressed, the distinction between immortality and mortality, is brought before us? One does not need to know that, intellectually. Rather, when a human being stands before this picture that mirrors the very meaning of the world, the experience penetrates the soul with magical force. Nor did the painter need to be an occultist in order to paint it. Nevertheless, powers existed in Leonardo's soul that could bring to expression precisely this highest, most significant meaning. That is why the greatest works of art have such a powerful effect; they are deeply linked with the meaning of the cosmic order. In earlier times, artists were connected to the significance of the cosmic order in dim consciousness without knowing it. But art would perish, it would not be able to continue, were it not that, in the future, spiritual science as a new form of knowledge will bring a new foundation to the arts.

Unconscious art has become a thing of the past. Art that allows itself to be inspired by spiritual science stands at the beginning of its development. Although artists in the past did not need to know what stood at the basis of their art works, artists in the future will have to know, but they will have to know by means of powers that can once again portray immortality—powers that can present something out of the full content of the soul. For whoever tries to make spiritual science an intellectual science expressed in schemes and paradigms does not understand it. But whoever with all the concepts we have developed here—such as sacrifice, bestowing virtue and renunciation—experiences with every word what seeks to spring forth from the word, the idea, itself—experiencing what flows out of the many-sided nature of the pictures—that individual understands spiritual science.

One can present schemes if one believes that the development of the world fulfills itself in abstract concepts. But, if one wishes to present such living concepts as sacrifice, bestowing virtue and resignation, schemes no longer suffice. These three words can be presented schematically—if only one does not think much beyond a few letters. But if we wish to consider these concepts—sacrifice, the virtue of bestowing, and renunciation—then we must paint pictures for ourselves such as those we described the last time: the sacrificing Thrones, who sent their sacrifice up to the Cherubim, who spread out the smoke of sacrifice, who received the light back from the Archangels, and so forth.

And when, in the next lecture, we move forward to consider the Moon existence, we shall see how the picture becomes richer. We shall see how the liquefying of the gathering cloud masses—which ripple as Moon mass—and the enchanting lightning of the Seraphim have to be added to it.† Then we shall have to try to reach a fuller understanding. About this, let me say: In the future, humankind will find how to create the possibility, the artistic material, the artistic means, to bring to expression in and for the outer world what otherwise may be read in the Akashic Chronicle.

4

THE INNER ASPECT OF THE
MOON EMBODIMENT OF THE EARTH

BERLIN, NOVEMBER 21, 1911†

We have pursued a difficult aspect of our worldview to the point where, to some extent, we have learned to see the spiritual reality that lies behind appearances in the outer, sensible world. Outwardly, however, appearances only very slightly betray the real fact that the characteristic form of the spiritual—as we experience it in our soul life—actually stands behind what we see in the sensible world. Yet we have come to recognize that spiritual activity, spiritual qualities and characteristics do indeed stand behind such appearances. For example, we now recognize that what appears to us in ordinary life as the quality of warmth, heat, or fire, is the spiritual expression of sacrifice. And in what we encounter as air—which, in our concepts, reveals so little that it is spiritual—we recognize what we call the bestowing virtue of particular cosmic beings. In water, we recognize what can be called resignation, renunciation.

In earlier worldviews—I mention this briefly—the existence of the spiritual within the outwardly material was, of course, more quickly intuited and recognized. Evidence of this may be seen in our habitual use today of the word *spirit*—which today we use in a particular way concerning what is spiritual—to refer to especially volatile substances. I say "spiritual" rather than "spirit." In the outer world, however, people do not necessarily apply the term *spiritual* to true spiritual reality or what is beyond the senses. As some of you know, a letter was once addressed to a Munich society of spiritualists and no one knew what a society of spiritualists was, so it was delivered to the main office of the merchants of "spirits," that is, alcoholic beverages.

To return to our theme: today we will look at the significant transition that occurred in the development of the planet Earth as evolution progressed from ancient Sun to ancient Moon. Thus, we will have to consider another kind of spiritual development.

We must begin with the point we took up in the last lecture—the act of renunciation. We saw last time that, in this renunciation or "forgoing," spiritual beings give up the opportunity to receive a sacrifice—a sacrifice that we recognized as the sacrifice of will or the will substance. When we imagine that certain beings wished to sacrifice their will substance and that higher beings declined to accept this will by their act of forgoing, then we will easily rise to the concept that this will substance—which these beings wished to sacrifice to higher spiritual beings—had to remain with the beings who wished to sacrifice it but were not allowed to do so. Thus, within the context of the cosmos, there are beings who were ready to present their sacrifice, that is, were prepared devoutly to surrender what reposes in their innermost being, but were not permitted to do so and therefore had to keep it within themselves. Or, to put it another way: because the sacrifice was rejected, these beings could not establish a certain bond with higher beings that would have come about had they been allowed to sacrifice.

Cain's confrontation with Abel in the Bible personifies and historically symbolizes some of the meaning of this "rejected sacrifice," albeit in an intensified way.† Cain also wanted to offer his sacrifice to his God. But his sacrifice was not found pleasing, and God would not accept it. Abel's sacrifice, on the other hand, was accepted by God. What we want to pay attention to here is Cain's inner experience when he discovered that his sacrifice was rejected. To reach the greatest possible degree of understanding in this matter, we must be clear that we should not introduce into the higher regions, of which we are speaking of here, ideas that have meaning only in ordinary life. It would be false to say that the rejection of the sacrifice came about through fault or wrongdoing. In these regions we cannot yet refer to sin and atonement as we are familiar with them in ordinary life. Rather, we have to view these beings from the perspective of the higher beings who refused the sacrifice. In other words, the higher beings were simply relinquishing or withdrawing their acceptance of the sacrifice. There is nothing that indicates any fault or failure in the mood of soul that we characterized last week. Rather, the act of surrender and resignation encompasses all that is great and meaningful. Yet, we can sense that, within those beings who wanted to offer the sacrifice, there did arise a mood that initiated something like opposition—even if it was extremely faint opposition—toward those beings who refused their sacrifice. Therefore, when this mood of opposition presents itself to us at a later time, as in the case of Cain, it is presented in a magnified manner. We will not find the same mood that we find in Cain also in those beings who developed during the transition from the Sun to the Moon. Among these beings, the mood of opposition occurs in a different degree. Again, we can come to know this mood in an authentic way only if we look into our own soul, as we did during the last lecture, and ask ourselves, where we can find such a mood in our own soul, and what soul conditions can make us aware of the mood that must have developed in the individuals whose gift of sacrifice had been rejected.

This mood in us—and here we come closer and closer to earthly human life—is actually familiar to every soul in its uncertainty, and at the same time in its torment or pain, in a way that I will address more fully in next Thursday's public lecture: "The Hidden Depths of Soul Life."† This mood or attitude, familiar to every soul, reigns in the secret depths of soul life and presses toward its surface where the mood—perhaps—creates the least torment. But we human beings often go around in this mood. Without being aware of it in our higher consciousness, we carry it within us. We may recall the words of the poet: "Only one who knows longing knows what I suffer."† These words capture the vague yet persistent torment of the soul that also carries a nuance of pain with it. What is meant here is longing as a mood of soul. This is longing as it lives continuously in the human soul—as a soul mood—and not just when the soul aspires to or strives for this or that.

In order to transport ourselves into what occurred spiritually in the evolutionary phases of ancient Saturn and the Sun, we had to raise our gaze to special conditions of the soul that start to appear when the human soul begins to strive and orient itself toward a higher striving. In the second lecture we tried to clarify the nature of surrender or sacrifice by drawing it out of our own soul life. We saw what a human being can achieve of the wisdom that we see trickling into and created out of what one could call: the "willingness to give" or the "readiness to surrender one's own self." The closer we approach the earthly circumstances that have developed out of earlier conditions, the more we encounter a mood of soul that is similar to what human beings today can still experience. But we must be clear that our whole soul life, insofar as our soul is inserted into an earthly body, lies like a top layer over a hidden soul life that flows in depths beneath its surface. Who could fail to know that there is a hidden life of soul? Life teaches us well enough that such a soul life exists.

In order to clarify something about this hidden life of the soul, let us assume that a child—let us say in the seventh or eighth year or at another time of life—experiences this or that. For example, having been blamed for doing something which, in fact, he or she did not do, a child may have experienced an injustice—children are often especially sensitive to this. Nevertheless, it was convenient for those around the child to settle the matter by blaming the child for doing this or that. Children, indeed, are acutely sensitive to suffering an injustice in this way. But life is such that, after this experience has eaten deeply into this young life, the following years added other layers to the soul's existence, and the child, at least in terms of everyday life, forgot the matter. Perhaps such a matter never again arises. But let us assume that at the age of fifteen or sixteen the young person, let us say at school, experiences a new injustice. And now, what otherwise lay at rest deep within the surging soul, begins to stir. The young person in question doesn't even need to know that a recollection of what was experienced in earlier years is at work, and may actually form completely different ideas and concepts. If what had occurred earlier had not taken place, however, then the young person would simply go home, shed a few tears, and perhaps also complain a bit, but would get over it. But since the earlier event did occur—here I emphasize very pointedly that the young person does not need to know what is happening—the earlier event works beneath the surface of the life of soul, just as beneath the smooth appearance of the ocean's surface waves may be surging. And what otherwise would have resulted only in tears, complaints, and insults, now becomes a student's suicide! Thus, from the deepest levels, the hidden depths of the soul life rise to the surface to play their role. And the most important force that rules in these depths—becoming most significant as it presses upward in its original form—and about which we nevertheless remain unconscious—is longing. We know the names that this force has in the outer world, but these are only vague, metaphoric names, because they express relationships that are complex and do not at all rise into consciousness.

Let us take a familiar phenomenon—those who live in the city may be less affected by it but even they nonetheless will have observed it in others—I mean, the feeling one describes as "homesickness." If you were to explore what homesickness really is, you would see that basically homesickness is something different for every human being. For one person it is this, for another person, something else. One person longs for the familiar tales listened to at home, never realizing that this is really a yearning for home—what lives within the individual is an unfocused longing, an undirected wishing. Another longs for a particular mountain, or—when watching rippling water—for the river that was often used for play in childhood. All these different qualities that are often unconsciously at work in the soul may be included in the term "homesickness" which expresses something that can be played out in thousands of different ways and yet is best described as a kind of longing. Even more indefinite are the yearnings that arise as perhaps the most tormenting ones in life. The human being is not aware longing is involved, but nevertheless that is what it is. But what is this longing? By bringing it into connection with the mood of the beings who wished to offer sacrifice but had to renounce their sacrifice, we have suggested that it is a kind of will and wherever we examine this longing, we can see that it is a type of will. But what kind of will is it? It is a will or intent that cannot be fulfilled, for, if it could be satisfied, the longing would cease. It is a will that cannot be realized—that is how we must define longing.

Thus, we would have to characterize the mood of those beings whose sacrifice was rejected somewhat as follows. What we can perceive in the depths of our soul life as longing is what remains in us as an inheritance from those ancient times we are now speaking of. Just as we receive other qualities as legacies from other ancient stages of development, so we receive from the Moon phase of evolution all forms of longing to be found in the depths of the soul, all forms of will that cannot be fulfilled, of will that is held in check. By turning back the sacrifice offered during this phase of development, beings with restrained, held-back wills were created. Because they had to restrain and keep this will within themselves, they were in a very special situation. And here, again, if one wishes to feel and experience these matters, one must transpose them into one's own condition of soul—for mere thoughts will scarcely suffice to penetrate these conditions.

A being who can sacrifice the will becomes, in a certain sense, united with the other being in relation to whom the sacrifice occurs. That, too, we can feel in human life—how we live and weave ourselves into a being to whom we bring a sacrifice; how fulfilled and happy we feel in the presence of that being. Here we are speaking of sacrifice to higher beings—encompassing, universal beings—to whom the sacrificing beings glance upward in utter delight. And for this reason, what is held back by the beings as restrained will, as longing, can never be the same as it would have been in inner mood—in inner soul content—as it would have been had they been allowed to complete their sacrifice. For if the sacrificing beings had been permitted to make their sacrifice, it would have become part of the other beings. We may say then, by way of comparison, that, if the Earth and the other planetary beings had been allowed to sacrifice to the Sun, then they would have been united with the Sun. But, if they were not permitted to sacrifice to the Sun and had to withhold what they would have sacrificed, then they would remain separate and draw their sacrifice back into themselves.

If we grasp what is now expressed in a single word, then we notice that something new has entered into the cosmic all. Understand clearly that it cannot be expressed in any other way: beings who would sacrifice to another all that lives within them, who would surrender themselves to a universal being—such beings, when the sacrifice is not accepted, are instructed to carry the sacrifice within themselves. Don't you feel that something flashes up here that we may call "ego" or "egoity," which later emerges as *egoism* in all of its forms? In this way we can feel that what flowed into evolution continued to live on as a legacy within those beings. Within longing we see egoism flashing like lightning, albeit in its weakest form; and we also see longing slipping into cosmic development. And thus we see how beings who surrender to longing, that is, surrender themselves to their egoism, are—if something else does not intervene—condemned in a certain way to one-sidedness, to living merely in themselves.

Let us imagine a being who has been permitted to sacrifice. This being lives in the other being—and forever lives in the other. A being who has not been permitted to sacrifice can live only within its own being, and thus such a being is excluded from all that would have been experienced in the other being—in this instance, in higher beings. In this case, in fact, the beings in question would have been taken out of the course of evolution, condemned, and banished to one-sidedness—had something not occurred that sought to enter the course of development to eliminate the one-sidedness. This "something" is the entry of new beings who prevent the condemnation and exile into one-sidedness. Just as in the instance of the Beings of Will on Saturn and the Beings of Wisdom on the Sun, so on the Moon we see the Spirits of Movement step forth. By this we are not imagining movement in space. Rather, by the term "movement" we refer to something that is more related to the process of thinking. Everyone knows the expression "movement of thought," although this refers just to the flow and the fluidity of one's own thinking. But even from this expression we can see that if we wish to gain a comprehensive grasp of movement, we must understand that movement is something other than merely changing position in space—that is just one aspect of movement. If a number of human beings are devoted to a higher being who expresses all that is in them because the higher being accepted all that was offered in sacrifice, then these human beings live and are fulfilled in that one being. If their sacrifices are rejected, however, these human beings must live within themselves and can never be fulfilled. Thus the Spirits of Movement enter and lead the beings who would otherwise have had to depend upon themselves into relationship with all of the other beings. The Spirits of Movement must not be thought of as beings who just bring about changes in location. Rather, they are beings who bring forth something whereby one being continuously comes into new relation to others.

We can form an idea of what is attained at this stage of the cosmos if we again reflect on the corresponding mood of soul. Who does not know what torment it is when longing comes to a halt, a standstill, and cannot experience change of any kind. It forces a person into the unbearable state we call boredom. But this boredom, which we usually attribute only to superficial people, has all manner of levels. This boredom even has levels that affect great and noble natures, in whom there lives what their own nature expresses as a longing that cannot be satisfied in the outer world. And what better way is there to satisfy this longing than through change? The evidence for this is that beings who feel this longing search continuously for relations with new beings. The anguish of the longing is often overcome through what is brought about by changed relations with constantly new sets of beings.

Thus, we see that while the Earth went through its Moon phase, the Spirits of Movement brought change, movement, and ever-renewing connections to new beings and situations into the lives of the yearning-filled beings who otherwise would have become desolate, for boredom is a kind of desolation. Movement in space from one place to another is only one aspect of this broad spectrum of movement of which we are speaking. We experience another kind of movement when, in the morning, we have a specific thought content in our soul that we do not have to keep to ourselves but can give to someone else. In this way, we overcome one-sidedness in our longing through variety, change, and movement in what we experience. What we have in external space is just a special kind of capacity for change.

Consider a planet facing the Sun. If the planet were always in the same position in relationship to the Sun, if it never moved, it would remain fixed in its one-sidedness. The planet would always turn just one side to the Sun. But then, to bring about a change in its position, the Spirits of Movement come and lead the planet around the Sun. A change in location is just one kind of change. And when the Spirits of Movement bring about change of location in the cosmos, they bring about a specific instance of the general phenomenon of movement.

Because the Spirits of Movement have introduced movement and change into the cosmos, something else has to come with it. We have seen in evolution—that is, in the whole cosmic multiplicity evolving in the form of the Spirits of Movement, Spirits of Personality, Spirits of Wisdom, Spirits of Will, and so forth—that substantiality is also present in the form of the bestowing virtue that streams toward radiating wisdom to form the spiritual basis of air and gas. This now flows together with the will that has been transformed into longing and, in these beings, becomes what human beings know—not yet as thought, but as *picture*. We can visualize this best with the image we have when dreaming. The fleeting, fluid dream picture can call forth an image of what occurs in a being in whom will lives as longing and who is led into relation with other beings by the Spirits of Movement. As a being is brought before another, the first being cannot entirely surrender itself to the other, for its own egoity lives within it. But the being in question can receive a fleeting picture of the other being—a picture that lives like a dream picture within it. In this way, what we may call the rising tide of images in the soul arises. In other words, picture consciousness came into being during this phase of development. And since we human beings ourselves went through this phase of development without our current earthly "I"-consciousness, we must imagine ourselves without what we attain today through our "I." In that period, we existed and wove within the cosmic all, while something lived within us that we can compare with our experience of longing.

In a certain way—if one forgot the conditions of suffering manifest on earth—one could imagine that suffering could not be other than the poet describes: "Only one who knows longing knows what I suffer." It was during the Moon phase that suffering and pain as manifestations of the soul came into our nature and into the nature of other beings who are bound up with our evolution. Thereafter the otherwise empty inner self—the inner self that suffers from longing—was filled with a healing balm in the form of picture consciousness poured into these natures through the activity of the Spirits of Movement. If this had not happened these Moon beings—Moon natures—would have been empty in their soul, empty of everything other than longing. But the balm of the pictures trickles in, fills the solitude and emptiness with manifoldness, and thus leads beings out of the state of exile and condemnation.

When we take such words seriously, we have both what lies spiritually at the foundation of what developed during the Moon phase of our Earth, and what now lies layered beneath the Earth phase in the deep recesses of our consciousness. But this lies so deep within the recesses of our soul—and I shall show this the day after tomorrow in a popular form in a public lecture[†]—that it can become active in these recesses without our being aware of it and then emerge into consciousness, just as surging waters in the ocean depths create waves on its surface. Beneath the surface of our ordinary "I"-consciousness we have a deep-seated soul life that can surge to the surface. And what does this soul life say when it comes to the surface? Once we understand the cosmic foundation of this unconscious life of the soul, we could say that our soul life, which we can feel rising out of the recesses of the soul, is a breaking-through of what was set in motion during the Moon phase of development, but first penetrated us during the Earth phase itself. And when we grasp the interplay of the Moon nature with our Earth nature, then we have the real explanation of what was brought over spiritually to Earth existence from the ancient Moon.

Keep in mind, as I have just described, that it was necessary for pictures to surface continuously in order to alleviate the desolation. If you do so, then a concept of great import and significance will come to you: namely, that the longing human soul in its yearning, tormented emptiness, satisfies and keeps this longing in harmony through the constant succession of pictures arising one after the other. And, after the images arise and remain a while, then the old longing dawns again in the recesses of the soul, and the Spirits of Movement call up new pictures. Then fresh images are present again for a while, until the longing for new pictures is once again renewed. The important statement we must make about this aspect of the life of the soul is that, if the longing is satisfied only through images that in turn constantly seek out new images, then there is no end to this infinite flow. The only way to intervene in this process is if something enters the unending flow of images that can redeem the longing with something other than pictures, that is, with realities. In other words, the phase of the planetary embodiment of our Earth in which images guided by the activity of the Spirits of Movement satisfy the longing must be replaced by the planetary phase of the Earth embodiment that we must call the phase of *redemption*. Indeed, as we shall see, the Earth may be called the "planet of redemption," just as the earlier embodiment of the Earth, Moon existence, may be called the "planet of longing," a longing that could be appeased, but only through a neverending process stretching to infinity. Throughout this life, while we live in earthly consciousness—which, as we have seen, brings before us the act of redemption through the Mystery of Golgotha—there arises out of the recesses of our soul that which continuously creates a longing for redemption. It is as if we had waves of ordinary consciousness at the surface of consciousness; and, beneath this, in the depths of the ocean of our soul life, the bedrock of our soul lived in the form of a longing; and this longing aspired ceaselessly to carry out the sacrifice to the universal being who can satisfy it—not just appease it with an infinite sequence of pictures, but fulfill it once and for all.

As earthly human beings, we can actually feel these moods. They are the best a person can experience. Indeed, those earthly human beings who today—in our time, above all—feel this longing are those who are coming toward our spiritual-scientific movement. In external life we learn to recognize everything that satisfies our ordinary, surface consciousness. Out of our unconsciousness, however, there pulses something that can never be satisfied by external particulars and longs for the central foundation of life. But we can attain this central basis only once we have a universal science that concerns itself with the totality of life, not just with particulars. What arises in the depths of the soul today—seeking to be brought into higher consciousness—must be brought into contact with universal existence that lives in the world. If this contact is not made then the longing for something unachievable arises out of the recesses of the soul.

Spiritual science, in this sense, is a response to the longings that live in the recesses of the soul. And, since everything that occurs in the world has its prelude in an earlier time, we should not be surprised that a person living today would want to subdue the power of this soul-longing through spiritual science—especially when such soul forces lie beyond conscious awareness and threaten to consume a person, as these longings do. In earlier times, when this spiritual wisdom did not exist and so was unobtainable, such a person would have wasted away with ever-present longing for spiritual wisdom and been denied the possibility of grasping the meaning of life—precisely because he or she was a "great spirit." Today, on the other hand, something can trickle into the soul that would ease the longing for images and drown out and silence the desolation. Earlier, a person could only long for a cessation of this march of images, and long for it all the more as the throng of images became increasingly persistent!

When we hear Heinrich von Kleist writing to a friend in the following way we can hear this expressed in the voice of someone who lived in an era when one could not yet attain this spiritual wisdom that pours itself out like balm into the longing of the soul:

> Who desires to be happy on this Earth? I would almost like to say, shame on you, if you want to be happy! What shortsightedness it is, O noble human being, to strive for such a goal here, where all ends in death. We meet, we love each other for three springs, and then, for an eternity, flee from each other. And yet what is the striving worth, when there is no love! Ah, there has to be something more than love, happiness, fame and x, y, z; something our souls do not even dream about.
>
> It cannot be an evil spirit who stands at the pinnacle of the world. It is just something incomprehensible. Do not we, too,

smile when children cry? Just think of this unending vastness! Myriad realms of time, each one a life, and each one a manifested existence such as this world of ours! What is the name of the little star we see when the heavens are clear and we gaze at Sirius? And this gigantic firmament is only a speck of dust in relation to infinity! O moment of stillness, tell me, is this a dream? Between two linden leaves, which we watch as we lie on our backs in the evening, lies a perspective, richer in intuitions than our thoughts can grasp and words can express. Come, let us do something good and die doing so! One of the millions of deaths we have already died and must yet die in the future. It is as if we go from one room into another. Look, the world appears to me as if it were all boxed up together, the small is just like the great!†

The longing expressed in these words drove this individuality to write to his friend in this way. But this spirit—Kleist—could not yet find a satisfaction for his longing in the way that modern souls can today when they approach spiritual science with energetic understanding. For this spirit is one who ended his life one hundred years ago when he shot, first his friend, Henriette Vogel, and then himself, and who now rests on the banks of the Wannsee, in the lonely grave that first enclosed his remains a century ago.†

It is a remarkable act of Providence—one would like to say, of karma—that we can speak here of what Kleist expresses, which best describes what we tried to say about the transformation of the withheld sacrifice of will into longing—the easing of which can occur through the Spirits of Movement and the impulse toward final satisfaction of longing, which may be attained on the "planet of redemption." It is a remarkable karmic resolution that, precisely on this day, we speak about what reminds us of a soul who brought this unfocused longing to expression in the most elevated language, and then poured this yearning into the most tragic deed in which the longing can be embodied. How can we fail to recognize that this man's spirit in its totality, as he stands before us, is actually a living embodiment of what lives deep within the soul and leads us back to an existence other than an earthly existence—if only we want to recognize it? Does not Kleist describe for us in the most meaningful way what a person can experience of what impels human beings to seek what lies beyond them—which, later, he would have comprehended if he had not prematurely severed the thread of his own life? Did he not experience just what you may find described in the first pages of *The Spiritual Guidance of the Individual and Humanity?*†

Think of von Kleist's drama *Penthesilea*.† How much more there is in Penthesilea than she can fathom with her own earthly consciousness!† We could not understand her in her particularity at all if we could not presume that her soul is infinitely more expansive than the narrow little soul that she—a great soul—encompasses with her earthly consciousness. Therefore, in the play, a situation must arise that artistically draws the unconscious into the drama. Thus, the possibility that the series of events—as Kleist sets them before Achilles—would be surveyed with higher consciousness must be prevented. Otherwise, we would not be able to experience the magnitude of the tragedy. Penthesilea is led captive to Achilles, but she is deluded into believing that Achilles is her prisoner. That is why reference is made to "her" Achilles. What lives in the aware consciousness must be plunged into nonconsciousness.

And what role does this lower consciousness play in a situation like the one portrayed in *Kätie of Heilbronn*,† especially with respect to the remarkable relationship between Katie and Wetter of Strahl, which is not carried out in full consciousness but in the deeper levels of the soul where powers reside that move from one person to another unbeknown to human beings. With this situation before us, we feel the spiritual nature of what lies within the ordinary forces of gravitation and attraction in the world. We feel what lies within the forces of the world. For example, in the scene where Katie stands facing her beloved, we see what lives beneath consciousness and how it is related to what lives externally in the world and to what one refers to dryly as the attracting powers of the planets. A century ago not even a penetrating, striving soul could plunge into this deeper level of consciousness. Today, it is possible to do so.

The tragedy of the *Prince of Homburg*† also strikes us in a completely different way today than it did a century ago. I would like to know how an abstract thinker who wishes to attribute everything a human being accomplishes to reason would explain a figure like the Prince of Homburg, who carried out all of his great deeds in a kind of dream state, even those deeds that finally led to victory. Indeed, Kleist clearly shows that the prince could not have achieved his victory out of his aware consciousness and that, with regard to higher consciousness, he was not a particularly distinguished person—for afterward he whimpered in the face of death. Only when what lived deep within his soul was drawn out by an extraordinary effort of will—only then—was the prince able to pull himself together.

What remains as a legacy for the human being out of the Moon consciousness is something that cannot be brought out by abstract science. It is something that must be derived from concepts that are many-sided, subtle, and capable of grasping spiritual matters with soft contours—that is, concepts such as are brought by spiritual science. The greatest concepts connect themselves to the intermediary and the ordinary ones.

Thus we see that spiritual science shows how conditions we experience in our soul today are connected to the cosmos and cosmic totality. We also understand how only what we experience in the soul can generate a concept of the spiritual foundation of things. Furthermore, we begin to comprehend that in our age it becomes possible to satisfy what the age preceding our own longed for, but which could only be given in our time. Thus, a kind of admiration arises for those human beings in a previous age who could not find their way to what their hearts longed for—the world could not give it to them. Truly, when we remind ourselves that all human life is a whole and that a person today can devote his or her life to spiritual movements that human beings long ago already had need of—as indeed their destinies show us—then a certain admiration for such individuals can arise.

And so we may point to spiritual science as a bearer of the redemption of human longing. Above all we may do so on a day that, since it is the centenary of the tragic death of one of these yearning individuals, is well suited to remind us that spiritual science now provides what tempestuous but also woeful human beings have sought for a long time. This is the thought—perhaps also the anthroposophical thought—that we can lay hold of on this hundredth anniversary of the death of one of the greatest German poets.

5

The Inner Aspect of the Earth Embodiment of the Earth

BERLIN, DECEMBER 5, 1911

So far in these lectures we have placed before our souls a series of observations showing that the spiritual stands behind everything that we call maya, or the great illusion. Today, let us ask ourselves once more: How do we come to know that behind all that surrounds us—from the perspective of our senses and our understanding of the cosmos as it is conveyed through our physical bodies—the spiritual is discernible?

We were able to characterize the spiritual in the course of our previous explorations because we insisted on putting aside the immediate, outward appearances of the world and penetrating the qualities of true reality, which we identified as the willingness to sacrifice, the virtue of bestowing, and resignation or renunciation—qualities we could come to know only if we looked into our own souls—qualities, in fact, that we could comprehend and receive *only* in the context of our own souls. In other words, if we want to understand those qualities that we presume embody what is real and true behind the world of illusion—and if we wish to understand them in their true nature—we must say: This world of true being or existence, this world of reality contains real, live qualities or characteristics that we may compare only with qualities we can perceive within our own soul. If, for example, we wish to characterize what expresses itself outwardly in the appearance of warmth—characterizing it in relationship to its true nature as sacrificial service, as sacrifice streaming into the world—we must lead the element of warmth back to the spiritual, at the same time eliminating the external veil of existence, thereby demonstrating that this quality in the outer world is recognizable as the same as our own spiritual nature.

Before continuing our observations we must consider another idea. Does everything that we find in the world of maya really disappear into a kind of nothingness? Is there really nothing in the world of sense perception and outward understanding that corresponds, as it were, to what is true or real?

The following would be a good comparison. We may say that, just as the inner powers of a stream—or, indeed, of the ocean itself—lie concealed within the watery mass, the world of truth or reality lies initially hidden. Therefore we may say that the world of maya may be compared with the rippling play of waves on the water's surface. The comparison is good because it shows us that something does indeed flow upward out of the depths of the ocean, causing the rippling waves on the surface. It shows us, too, that this something is the substantiality of the water and a certain configuration of its forces. But whether we use this or that comparison is unimportant. We still must pose the question: Is there something in the broad realm of maya that "really" exists?

Today, I want to proceed as we did in the previous lectures. We will gradually approach what we wish to place before our soul, taking soul experiences as our starting point. Having progressed spiritually through the Saturn, Sun, and Moon existences, we have now reached the Earth existence. Thus we shall begin with even more familiar—one could even say, more common—experiences of the soul than we did last time. Last time, we worked out of the hidden depths of soul life, out of what arises in what spiritual science calls our astral body. There, we felt longing stirring, and we saw how longing worked within a being—in this case, the human being. We saw, too, how such longing in soul life could be alleviated only in a world of pictures. We came to understand the world of pictures as the inner movement in soul life. And thereby we found our way from the microcosm of the individual soul to the macrocosm of world creation, which we attributed to the Spirits of Movement.

Today, then, I want to take as our starting point a familiar soul experience that was already known and alluded to ancient Greece, and is today still very meaningful in its truthfulness. This experience is hinted at in the words: All philosophy, that is, all striving toward a certain human knowledge, arises out of wonder.† This formulation is, in fact, correct. Whoever reflects a little and pays attention to the process one experiences in one's soul as one approaches some kind of learning will already have discovered that a healthy path to knowledge always has its origin in wonder or in wondering about something. Amazement and wonder—out of which all learning processes arise—belong precisely among those soul experiences that elevate and bring life to all that is dull, empty, and dry. For what sort of knowledge would it be that took a place in our soul, yet did not arise from wonder? It would certainly be a kind of knowledge that was immersed in emptiness and pedantry. Only that soul process leading from wonder to the bliss we experience in solving a riddle—thus raising itself beyond wonder—only that soul process beginning in wonder ennobles and gives inner liveliness to learning. You should actually try to feel the dryness of knowledge that is not saturated with these inner feelings. The context of true, healthy knowledge is the wonder and delight that solving a riddle engenders. Other kinds of knowledge can be acquired from outside and can be applied on some basis or other. Nevertheless, in all seriousness, any knowledge that is not embraced by these two feelings does not really spring from the human soul. All the "aroma" of knowledge that the atmosphere of the living element in knowledge creates arises out of these two things—wonder, and delight over gratified wonder.

But what kind of origin does wonder itself have? Why does wonder, that is, amazement about something external, arise in the soul? Wonder and astonishment arise because we stand before some being or thing or fact and feel strangely delighted by it. This strangeness is the first element that leads to wonder and surprise. But we do not feel wonder or amazement about everything that is strange to us. We experience wonder toward something strange only if, at the same time, we also feel related to it. We could describe this feeling as follows: There is something in this thing or being that is not yet a part of me, but which could become a part of me. When we perceive something with wonder and astonishment we feel that it is strange, and at the same time related to us.

This word *wonder* is connected with the word *astonishment*. Something is added to the phenomenon of wonder to which one can find no cognitive relationship. But that can only be the fault of the individual—at least the responsibility ought to rest with the person. And a person would not approach that something "wondrous" in a spirit of rejection or denial unless he or she had concluded that the thing or event *ought* to be related to him or her. For why do those who operate out of materialistic or purely intellectual concepts deny, for example, what others recognize as a wonder, if they do not have direct evidence that it is a lie or an untruth? Even philosophers today have to admit that one can never prove on the basis of phenomena spread out before humanity in the world that the Christ who incarnated in Jesus of Nazareth was not resurrected from the dead. Arguments can be made against this assertion. But what are these arguments? In terms of logic they are untenable. Enlightened philosophers today already admit that. For the arguments that can be brought forward on the materialistic side—for example, that no one until now has seen anyone arise from the dead as Christ arose from the dead—these arguments are logically at the same level as the argument that someone who had only seen fish must conclude that there are no birds. One can never derive in a logically consistent way, on the basis of the existence of one class of beings, that other beings do not exist. Likewise, one cannot derive anything about the event at Golgotha—which must be described as a "wonder"—on the basis of human experiences on the physical plane. However, if you tell someone about something that one would have to call a "miracle" (even though it were true), and the person says, "I cannot understand it," then that person is not opposing what we have said about the concept of astonishment, because this person is, in fact, showing that this same starting point for all knowledge also holds true for him- or herself. That person is demanding that your statement find an echo within him- or herself.

In a certain sense, this individual wants to own, spiritually or cognitively, what is being communicated, and, since that person does not believe this is possible, and that it has no relationship to him or her, such a person declines to accept it. Although we can arrive at the concept of "wonder" on our own, we should also acknowledge that amazement and astonishment—from the perspective of all ancient Greek philosophy—arise when human beings come face to face with something strange and yet must time recognize at the same something related or familiar there.

Let us now try to build a bridge between these concepts and those that we brought before our souls last time.

We demonstrated last time how a certain advance in evolution was brought about by beings who were ready to offer sacrifices, and by other beings' refusal to receive these offerings, and the return of the sacrifices to the beings who offered them. We recognized in the returned sacrifices one of the main factors in ancient Moon development. Indeed, one of the most significant aspects of ancient Moon development is that certain beings brought sacrifices to higher beings, who then returned the sacrifices; because of this, as the smoke from the offering of the Moon beings pressed upward toward the higher beings who would not accept the sacrifices, the smoke was guided back as substance into the beings who had wanted to offer the sacrifice. We have seen, too, that the beings of the ancient Moon are most distinctive in that they felt pressing back into themselves what they had wished to send up to higher beings as the substance of sacrifice.

Yes, truly, we have seen that the substance that sought to become part of the higher beings but was not able to do so remained behind in the very beings who sent it forth; and that thereby the capacity for longing arose in these beings who had offered a sacrifice that was rejected. Indeed, we have even now, in all that we experience as longing in our own soul, a legacy of the event on the ancient Moon—a legacy from beings who discovered that their sacrifice had not been accepted. The whole character of ancient Moon development, its spiritual atmosphere, when understood from a spiritual perspective, may be characterized by the fact that beings existed then who wished to present their sacrifice, but found that their offering was not accepted because the higher beings waived any claim to the sacrifice. Such is the peculiarly melancholic cause behind the characteristic atmosphere of the ancient Moon: rejected sacrifice. And Cain's rejected sacrifice, which points symbolically to the starting point for the evolution of earthly humankind, appears as a kind of recapitulation of this fundamental principle in ancient Moon development that took hold of Cain's soul—Cain, who also saw that his sacrifice was not accepted. Just as in the case of the beings of ancient Moon existence, such a rejection is something that can create a sorrow, a pain, in us that gives birth to longing.

We saw last time that the entry of the Spirits of Movement on the ancient Moon created a balance or redress between this rejected sacrifice and the longing that arose in the beings when the sacrifice was not accepted. At least the possibility was created whereby the longing that arose in the beings whose sacrifice was rejected could be satisfied to some extent. Imagine, in the most lively way, the following:

You have the higher beings to whom sacrifice should be given but who sent back the substance of the sacrifice. Longing arises in those beings who wanted to make the sacrifice and now feel: "If I had been able to give my sacrifice to the higher beings, the best of my own being would be living in those beings. Indeed, I myself would be living within those higher beings. But because I have been excluded from these beings, I stand here, and the higher beings stand over there!" The Spirits of Movement, however (and we should understand this almost literally) now bring these beings—in whom longing from the rejected sacrifice gleams toward the higher beings—into positions from which they can approach the higher beings from many different sides. And what rests in these beings as rejected offering is balanced, compensated for, by the wealth of impressions received from the higher beings encircling those who offered the rejected sacrifice. Thus a relationship is created between the beings who wished to offer the sacrifice and the higher beings who rejected it. And what remained unsatisfied because of the return of the offering can be compensated for in their new relation—so that it is as if the sacrifice had been accepted.

We can clarify what is meant here if we visualize the higher beings symbolically as the Sun and then, in a single position, the lesser beings gathered together as a planet. Let us suppose that the beings of the lesser planet wished to present their sacrifice to the higher planet, that is, to the Sun. But the Sun returned it, and the substance of the sacrifice must remain with the beings who offered the sacrifice. In their solitude and separation, these beings are filled with longing. Then the Spirits of Movement bring them into a circuit moving around the higher beings. Instead of sending forth a flow of the substance of sacrifice directly to the higher beings, it is possible for the beings who now contain the sacrifice within themselves to bring the substance into movement *around* the higher beings, thereby bringing the sacrifice into relation with the beings of a higher nature. It is just as if a person cannot appease a profound longing through one great fulfillment, but experiences instead a series of partial gratifications. That person's whole soul is brought into motion by such a series of partial gratifications. We described this very precisely the last time. We saw that because a being cannot feel inwardly united with the higher beings in sacrifice, impressions coming from without arise as a substitute. These substitute gratifications show us how such beings are able to achieve partial satisfaction.

Yet it is undeniable that the intended sacrifice would have had a different form in the higher beings than it had when it remained within the lower beings. For the actual conditions necessary for that intended form of existence lay in the higher beings. The conditions of existence in the lower beings are different from those within the higher beings. Once again, we can imagine this pictorially. If the entire substance of a planet flowed into the Sun, and the Sun did not reject it, the beings of this planet, as Sun beings, would discover different conditions of existence than they would if the Sun had returned the substance back to the planet. An alienation of what we must call the content of the sacrifice takes place through its rejection—an alienation of this substance of the sacrifice from its origin.

Consider this thought. Beings are forced to retain something within themselves that they would gladly present as a sacrifice and that they feel could fulfill its true purpose only if it could be presented as an offering. If you could recreate the experience of such beings you would have what one may call "the exclusion of a certain portion of cosmic beings from their own essential meaning and great cosmic purpose." Beings have something within themselves that would actually—if we may speak pictorially—only fulfill its purpose in another place. Consequently, this displacement of the rejected sacrifice's smoke—this displacement of the rejected substance of sacrifice—removes this sacrificial substance from the course of the rest of the cosmic processes.

If you grasp this thought not just with your intellect—for the intellect does not work in such matters—but if you grasp what is being expressed with your feeling, you will experience something like being torn out of the universal cosmic process. For the beings who rejected the sacrifice, it is just something they have pushed away from themselves. But for the other beings, those in whom the substance of the sacrifice remains, it is something that bears the imprint of alienation from one's own origin. Here, then, we have beings whose substantiality expresses alienation from one's origins. If one understands this sensitively—if one places sensitively before one's soul this idea of something in which alienation from its origins dwells—then one has the idea of death. Death in the universe is nothing other than what had to occur within the beings whose sacrifice was rejected and who had to retain that sacrifice within themselves. Thus we advance from resignation and renunciation, which we found in the third stage of evolution, to what was refused by the higher beings: death. And the true meaning of death is nothing other than the state of not being in one's true place, of being excluded from one's true place.

Even when death occurs concretely in human life, the same principle holds true. For when we look at a corpse left in the world of maya, it consists only of a substantiality that has been separated at the moment of death from the "I," the astral body, and the etheric body and has thereby been alienated from what gave it, as physical body, its only real significance. For the physical body of a human being has no meaning without the etheric body, the astral body, and the "I." At the moment of death, the physical body becomes meaningless; it is excluded from its source of meaning. When a person dies, what is no longer sense-perceptible presents itself to us in the macrocosm.

Because cosmic beings in higher spheres gave back what was intended to be brought to them as sacrifice, this rejected substance of sacrifice became subject to death—for death is the exclusion of cosmic substance or a cosmic being from its true purpose.

With this, we come to the spiritual nature of what we call the fourth element in the universe. If fire is in the purest sense sacrifice—and wherever fire or warmth occurs sacrifice lies spiritually behind it; if, behind everything that is spread out around our Earth as air, we discover gift-granting or bestowing virtue; if we can characterize flowing water, that is, the fluid element, as spiritual resignation or renunciation; then we must characterize the element of earth as the only bearer of death, as that which has been alienated from its meaning through rejection. Death would not exist if there were no element of earth. Here you have in concrete form something that shows how the solid arises out of the fluid. And this, too, in a certain way, reflects a spiritual process. Imagine, for instance, that ice forms in a pond, thus making the water become solid. What causes the water to turn to ice in fact cuts the water off from what gives it meaning as water. In this process you have the spiritual manifestation of becoming solid—the spiritual manifestation of becoming earth. For, with regard to the characteristics of the four elements, ice is, actually, earth; only what is fluid is water. Being separated from one's purpose and meaning is what we call death, and death presents and fulfills itself in the element of earth.

We began by posing the question whether anything real could be found in our world of maya, whether anything within it corresponds to reality. Consider very carefully the concept we have now placed before our soul. I told you at the beginning that the concepts in these lectures are rather complicated. Therefore, we must not just accept them intellectually. We must meditate upon them. Only then will they become clear to us. Let us take this concept of death, that is, the concept of what is Earth-related—for it presents a truly remarkable aspect. Of all the other concepts that we dealt with we had to say that there is no reality in what we find around us in the world of maya, that what is true is only to be found in the fundamentally spiritual. But here we have ascertained that something in the sphere of maya characterizes itself as death—precisely because it is separated from its purpose and because it actually ought to be in the spiritual realm. In other words: something is cut off and confined within this maya. It actually should not be there. Throughout the entire vast realm of maya we have only deceptions and illusions. Nevertheless, we do find something in maya that corresponds to what is true: namely, that in the moment something true is cut off from what gives it meaning in the spiritual it becomes subject to destruction and death. Here we have nothing less than the great truth that, *within the world of maya the only thing that shows itself in its reality is death!* All other appearances we must trace back to their reality; what is true lies behind all other appearances that arise in maya. In maya only death is to be found in its reality, for it consists of what is separated from the real and taken into maya. Thus, in the whole sphere of maya, death is the only reality.

And so, if we turn from what spreads out everywhere in universal maya to the great principles of the cosmos, a most important, most pertinent consequence presents itself for spiritual science in the following proposition: In our world of maya only death actually exists as something real.

We can also approach what I want to say here from another side. We can, for example, consider the beings of other realms that are here around us. We can ask: Do minerals, for example, die? For the esotericist it is meaningless to say that minerals die. For that would be similar to saying that a fingernail that has been cut has died. The fingernail is not something that in and of itself has a right to its own existence. It is a part of us, and when we cut the nail, we separate it from us and tear it away from the life it shared with us. It dies only when we ourselves die. In the same sense, for spiritual science, minerals do not die. For minerals are only members of a great organism, just as the fingernail is a member of our organism; and when a mineral seems to be destroyed, it is merely torn from the greater organism, as the piece of fingernail is separated from our organism when we cut it. The destruction of minerals is not death, for a mineral does not live in and of itself, rather it lives within the greater organism of which it is a member.

If you recall my lecture on the nature of plants,† you will know that the plant as such is not independent, either. The plant, too, is a member of the entire Earth organism, but not quite in the way that minerals are part of a larger organism. From a spiritual-scientific point of view it is meaningless to speak of the life of an individual plant; one must rather speak of the Earth organism, for plants are everywhere parts of this organism. When we come to the death of plants, the situation is similar to cutting a fingernail. We cannot say that the fingernail has died. The same is true of plants, for they belong to the greater organism, which is identical with the entire Earth. The Earth is an organism. It goes to sleep in spring, sending the plants, as its organs, out toward the Sun. In fall, the Earth reawakens and spiritually receives the plants back into itself by accepting their seeds into its being. It is meaningless to view the plants individually, for the Earth organism as a whole does not die, even though individual plants wilt. Similarly, when our hair turns gray, we do not die, even though we cannot turn our gray hair black again—at least, not by any natural means. Of course, we are in a different position than the plants. But the Earth may be compared to a human being who can turn gray hair back into black hair. The Earth itself does not die. What we see in wilting plants is a process that takes place on the Earth's surface. Although they wilt, however, we can never say that plants truly die.

Neither can we say of the animals that they die as we do. For the individual animal does not truly exist—only the group soul of the animal exists within the supersensible. What the animal really is, its true existence, exists only on the astral plane as the group soul: the individual animal is densified out of the group soul. And when the animal dies, it is set aside as a member of the group soul and is then replaced by another.

What we encounter as death in the mineral, plant, and animal realms is therefore only the semblance, the illusion of death. In reality, only the human being dies, for the human being has developed individuality so far that it descends into the physical body, in which a person must carry out an earthly existence in order to be real. Death has meaning only for the human being during earthly existence.

To grasp this, we must say: *Only human beings can actually experience death.* Moreover, as we learn from spiritual-scientific research, only human beings can really overcome death. Only for us is true victory over death possible. For all other beings, death is only apparent—it does not really exist. If we were to ascend beyond humanity to beings of the higher hierarchies, we would discover that the higher beings do not know death in the human sense. True death, that is, death in the physical realm, is only experienced by those beings who have to draw something out of existence in the physical plane. Human beings must achieve "I"-consciousness in the physical context. And that cannot be found without death. Neither for beings who stand in rank below the human being, nor for beings who stand above the human being, is it meaningful to speak of death. On the other hand, there is no undoing the most significant earthly deed of the being whom we call the Christ Being. Indeed, with regard to the Christ Being, we have seen that the Mystery of Golgotha—the victory of life over death—becomes the most important event of all. And where can this victory over death be carried out? Can it occur in higher worlds? No! For among the lower beings to whom we referred in the mineral, plant, and animal realms, we cannot speak of death because these beings actually have their true being in the higher world beyond the senses. And with regard to higher beings one cannot speak of death, but only of transformation, metamorphosis, and reordering. The incision into life that we call death occurs only with the human state. And human beings can experience death only in the physical context. If human beings had never entered the physical plane, they would never have known death, for a being who has not entered the physical plane knows nothing of death. There is nothing in other worlds that may be called death—in other worlds there is only transformation and metamorphosis. If the Christ had to go through death, then he had to descend to the physical realm! For he could experience death only in the physical realm.

Thus we see that the reality of higher worlds works in maya in a remarkable way in the historical development of the human being. If we are thinking of historical events in the right way, we must realize that although an event occurs in the physical realm, its source lies in the spiritual world. This is true of all historical events—*except one!* For we cannot say of the event at Golgotha that it occurred on the physical plane and something corresponding to it exists in a higher world. True, Christ himself belongs to the higher world and descended to the physical plane. But an archetype, such as we have for all other historical events, does not exist for what was accomplished at Golgotha. The Mystery of Golgotha could occur only in the physical realm.

Evidence for this will be provided out of spiritual science. For instance, in the course of the next three thousand years, there will be many new examples of the event at Damascus. We have often spoken of this. Human beings will develop capacities so that they will be able to perceive the Christ on the astral plane as an etheric figure, as Paul did at Damascus.† This experience of perceiving Christ through higher capacities—which will develop more and more among human beings in the course of the next three millennia, will begin in our twentieth century. From this time onward these capacities will gradually emerge, and over the next millennia they will be cultivated by a great number of human beings. That is, many people will come to know that Christ is a reality—that he lives—*by looking into higher worlds.* They will become acquainted with him, *as he lives now.* Nor will they become acquainted only with how he now lives, rather they will become convinced—precisely as Paul was—that he died and rose again. The basis for this, however, cannot be found in higher worlds, it must be found on the physical plane.

If a person today comes to understand and grasp how Christ's own development progresses and how, with it, certain human capacities also develop—if a person understands this through spiritual science—then there is nothing to prevent this person, when they pass through the portal of death, from participating in the Damascus event—for death now actually manifests as an initial shining forth of Christ into the world of humanity. Those who prepares themselves today for this event while in the physical body can also experience it in the life between death and new birth. Those, however, who do not prepare themselves for it—who gain no understanding of it in this incarnation—can know nothing, during the life between death and a new birth, of what is already happening now and, for the next three thousand years, will continue to happen in relation to Christ. They will have to wait until they are incarnated again. Then, when they are on Earth again, they will have to make further preparation for it. The death on Golgotha and what was created out of that death—which was needed to bring about the whole of Christ's subsequent development on Earth—can be grasped only in the physical body. It is the only important fact for our higher life that must be grasped in the physical body. Once understood in the physical body, it will be worked on further, cultivated more, in the higher worlds. But first it must be understood in the physical body. The Mystery of Golgotha could never have occurred in the higher worlds and has no archetype in the higher worlds. It is an event that encompasses a death confined entirely within the physical realm.

Therefore, it can only be understood within the context of the physical plane. Yes, it is one of the tasks of the human being on Earth to achieve this understanding in one of his or her incarnations.

Here we must say, therefore, that we have found something significant on the physical plane that demonstrates an immediate reality, an immediate truth. What is it that is real on the physical plane? What on the physical plane is so real that we stop short and say: "Here we have something that is true!" It is death in the world of humankind; but not death in the other realms of nature. To understand the historical events that occur in the course of earthly evolution, we must rise from the historical event to the spiritual archetype. But this is not the case with the Mystery of Golgotha. In the Mystery of Golgotha we have something that belongs immediately and directly to the world of reality.

The other side of what has just been said also manifests itself. This is extraordinarily interesting. It is most significant that we find that the event at Golgotha is denied nowadays to be a real event and that, if we are talking of outward history, people say that it is impossible to prove this event as historical fact. Among momentous historical facts, there is rarely one that is so difficult to prove through external, historically verifiable, means as the Mystery of Golgotha. Compared to this, think how easy it is to work with the historical arguments for the existence of a Socrates or a Plato or some other Greek figure who is important for the progress of humanity in the outer world. Still, many people—up to a certain point, justifiably—say: You cannot claim on the basis of history that Jesus of Nazareth actually lived! And yet, contrary historical evidence does not exist. Nevertheless, it is true, one cannot deal with the fact of the Mystery of Golgotha in the way that one deals with other historical facts.

It is most remarkable that this event, which occurred on the outer physical plane, shares a common characteristic with all facts of the supersensible realm: namely, that it does not allow itself to be proven in any outward way. And many of those people who deny the supersensible world are the same ones who lack the capacity to grasp this event—which is not at all a supersensible one. In fact, the reality of the event is supported by the effects it produces. Yet people suppose that these effects can occur without the real event itself actually having occurred historically. They explain that the effects are a consequence of sociological circumstances. But for someone who is familiar with the course of cosmic creation, the idea that the effects of Christianity could have occurred without a force standing behind them is about as clever as saying that cabbages can grow in a field without planting seeds.

We can go even further and say that for the individuals who participated in the compilation of the Gospels there was likewise no possibility of proving the historical event of the Mystery of Golgotha as a historical fact based on historical evidence—for it took place without leaving traces perceivable by outward observation. Do you know how the compilers of the Gospels, with the exception of the author of the Gospel of St. John—who was a direct witness of these events—became convinced of the truth of these events? They were not persuaded by historical sources, for they had nothing more than the oral tradition and the books of the Mysteries. These circumstances are outlined in my *Christianity as Mystical Fact*. They convinced themselves of the actual existence of Christ Jesus through the constellations of the stars, for they were still very learned about the relationship of the macrocosm to the microcosm. They had the knowledge—one can also have it today—with which one can calculate a significant point in world history through the constellations of the stars. They could say: "When the constellations are thus and so, then that being who is described as the Christ must have lived on Earth." In this way the authors of the Gospels of St. Matthew, St. Mark, and St. Luke were persuaded about the historical events. They gained the substance of the Gospels through clairvoyance, but the conviction that this or that could have occurred on Earth was drawn out of the constellations in the macrocosm. Anyone who knows this must believe the authors of the Gospels. Proving the inaccuracy of objections to the historicity of the Gospels is a thankless task. As anthroposophists, we must be clear that we place ourselves on an entirely different basis—the basis obtainable through insight into spiritual science.

In this regard, I would also like to draw attention to something that I have tried to establish during these lectures. The realities of which Anthroposophy speaks cannot be undermined or struck down by objections that are in and of themselves correct. Human beings can say a great deal that is correct according to their knowledge; that does not disprove spiritual science. In the lecture "How Does One Substantiate Theosophy?"† I drew a comparison and said: A little boy used to go into the village to get rolls for his family for breakfast. Now, in that village a roll cost two kreuzers and the boy was always given ten kreuzers. The boy brought home a number of rolls from the baker—one should note here that he was not a great arithmetician—and thought nothing more about it. Then a foster son was taken into the family, and he was sent to get the rolls from the baker instead of the other boy. The foster son was a good arithmetician, and so he said to himself: "You go to buy rolls and take ten kreuzers with you. A roll costs two kreuzers, and since ten divided by two equals five, you should bring home five rolls." But upon returning home, the boy discovered that he had brought six rolls. He said to himself: "That's wrong! You can't buy that many rolls for ten kreuzers, and since the addition is correct, tomorrow I expect to bring back five rolls." On the next day he received again ten kreuzers and again brought back six rolls. The addition was correct, but it did not correspond to the reality, for in fact the reality was different. It was the custom in that village, that whoever bought ten kreuzers worth of rolls received an extra roll, that is, one received six rolls instead of five. The boy's calculation was correct, but still it did not correspond to the reality.

Thus, the most critically thought-through objections to spiritual science can be "correct," but they may not have anything to do with the reality, which may stand on quite different principles. This is a wonderful example with which to demonstrate, even theoretically, the difference between what is arithmetically correct and what is actually true.

Thus, our efforts have shown that the world of maya leads back to reality. This process has shown us that fire is sacrifice, that the airy element is flowing, giving, bestowing virtue, that everything fluid is the result of renunciation, resignation. Today, we have added to these three truths a fourth: that the true nature of the earth or solid element is death, the separation of a substance from its cosmic purpose. When this state of separation was initiated, death itself entered as a reality into the world of maya or illusion. The gods themselves could never know death unless they descended in some way into the physical world, so as to understand death in its true nature in the physical world, the world of maya.

This is what I wanted to add to the concepts that we have discussed. Again, note that we can gain clarity about these concepts— so necessary, as we shall see, for a fundamental understanding of what is in the Gospel of Saint Mark—only through disciplined meditation, and by allowing them repeatedly to influence our soul.[†] For the Gospel of Mark can be understood only if one lays a foundation in the most significant cosmic concepts.

REFERENCE NOTES

Page 1, "we shall have to master some concepts ... other than those we have spoken of so far."
See Rudolf Steiner, *Background to the Gospel of St. Mark* (CW 124) (Hudson, NY: Anthroposophic Press, 1985) 10 lectures, Berlin, October 17, 1910-June 10, 1911.

Page 1, "esoteric observations concerning human evolution."
See, for instance, Rudolf Steiner, *Cosmic Memory* (CW 11) (Blauvelt, NY: Garber Books, 2006) written 1904-1908; *Rosicrucian Wisdom* (CW 99) (London: Rudolf Steiner Press, 2000) 14 lectures, Munich, May 22-June 6, 1907; *Universe, Earth and Man* (CW 105) (London: Rudolf Steiner Press, 1987), 11 lectures, Stuttgart, August 4-16, 1908.

Page 2, "Akashic Chronicle"
Cf. Rudolf Steiner, *Rosicrucian Wisdom* (CW 99) (London: Rudolf Steiner Press, 2000) 14 lectures, Munich, May 22-June 6, 1907. In lecture 4: "What is the Akashic Chronicle? We can form the truest conception of it by realizing that what comes to pass on our earth makes a lasting impression upon certain delicate essences, an impression that can be discovered by a seer who has attained Initiation. It is not an ordinary but a living Chronicle. Suppose a human being lived in the first century after Christ; what he thought, felt, and willed in those days, what passed into deeds—this is not obliterated but preserved in this delicate essence. The seer can behold it—not as if it were recorded in a history book, but as it actually happened."

Page 3, "Wilhelm Wundt"
Wilhelm Wundt (1832-1920), German physiologist, psychologist, and philosopher, founded the first Institute for Experimental Psychology in Leipzig (1879).

Page 3, "soul theory without soul"
The phrase "soul theory without soul" was coined by Friedrich Albert Lange (1828-1875) in the second volume of his *Geschichte des Materialismus (History of Materialism)* (1866).

Page 3, "Guardian of the Threshold"
The expression "Guardian of the Threshold" appears in a novel published in 1842 by Sir Edward Bulwer-Lytton (1803-1873), *Zanoni: A Rosicrucian Tale* (Blauvelt, NY: Garber Communications, 1989). For Rudolf Steiner's description, see *How to Know Higher Worlds* (CW 10) (Hudson, NY: Anthroposophic Press, 1994) written 1904-1905, and *A Way of Self-Knowledge and The Threshold of the Spiritual World*, translated and introduced by Christopher Bamford,

(CW 16/17) (Great Barrington, MA: Steiner Books, The Collected Works of Rudolf Steiner, 2006) written 1912 and 1913 respectively. The titles in German are: *Ein Weg zur Selbsterkenntnis des Menschen in acht Meditationen (A Way to Human Self-Knowledge: Eight Meditations)* (1912) and *Die Schwelle der geistigen Welt: Aphoristische Ausfuehrungen (The Threshold of the Spiritual World: Aphoristic Comments)* (1913).

Page 5, "Karl Rosenkranz"
Karl Rosenkranz (1805-1879), philosopher and biographer of Georg Wilhelm Friedrich Hegel (1770-1831). See his *Aus einem Tagebuch: Koenigsberg Herbst 1833 bis Fruehjahr 1846* (Leipzig, 1854), p. 24f.

Page 6, "How to Know Higher Worlds"
Rudolf Steiner, *How to Know Higher Worlds* (CW 10) (Hudson, NY: Anthroposophic Press, 1994) written 1904-1905; *Theosophy* (CW 9) (Hudson, NY: Anthroposophic Press, 1994) written 1904; *Stages of Higher Knowledge* (CW 12) (Spring Valley, NY: Anthroposophic Press, 1974) written 1905-1908; *An Outline of Esoteric Science* (CW 13) (Hudson, NY: Anthroposophic Press, 1997) written 1910; *A Way of Self-Knowledge and The Threshold of the Spiritual World* (CW 16/17) (Great Barrington, MA: Steiner Books, The Collected Works of Rudolf Steiner, 2006) written 1912 and 1913 respectively.

Page 12, "Albert Schwegler's ... book"
Albert Schwegler (1819-1857), philosopher and classicist. His *Geschichte der Philosophie im Umriss* was first published in Stuttgart in 1848.

Page 12, "Jacob Boehme"
Jacob Boehme (1575-1624) settled in Goerlitz as a shoemaker in 1594. In 1600, he was granted a profound mystical experience while polishing a pewter mug. For the remainder of his life, he sought to put what he had learned into language. A great mystic, philosopher, Sophiologist, and theosophist, Boehme drew deeply on Paracelsian alchemy (Theophrastus Bombastus Paracelsus von Hohenheim, 1493-1541) and Kabalistic as well as Christian esoteric traditions, and created a body of work that was to influence diverse strands of the Western tradition, including the theology of the Pietists and Quakers, Romanticism, German idealism (particularly Friedrich Schelling (1775-1854), *The System of Transcendental Idealism*, 1803), Russian philosophy, and twentieth-century existentialist theologians and philosophers such as Paul Tillich (1886-1965) and Nikolai Berdyaev (1874-1948). See Rudolf Steiner, *Mysticism after Modernism: Discovering the Seeds of a New Science in the Renaissance* (CW 7) (Great Barrington, MA: Anthroposophic Press, 2000), written 1901. The German title is: *Die Mystik im Aufgange des neuzeitlichen Geisteslebens und ihr Verhaeltnis zur modernen Weltanschauung*.

Page 25, "Archangels—Messengers of Beginning"
Archangeloi in Greek: *archai* = beginning, origin; *angeloi* = messengers.

Page 25, Dionysius the Areopagite"
Dionysius the Areopagite, a member of the Athenian Areopagus, was converted to Christianity by Paul (Acts 17:34). The text referred to here, *On the Heavenly Hierarchies*, was published under his name in Syria around 500 C.E. See *Dionysios Areopagita, Die Hierarchie der Engle und der Kirche* (Munich, 1955). Regarding the authenticity of this work, see Rudolf Steiner, *Christianity as Mystical Fact* (CW 8) (Great Barrington, MA: Steiner Books, The Collected Works of Rudolf Steiner, 2006) written 1902.

Page 33, "beings who remained behind in the course of development"
See, for instance, Rudolf Steiner, *The Spiritual Guidance of the Individual and of Humanity* (CW 15) (Hudson, NY: Anthroposophic Press, 1991) 3 lectures, Copenhagen, June 6-8, 1911, afterwards compiled in written form by Steiner and published in August 1911.

Page 40, "I would like to remind you of the Spanish king..."
King Alfons X of Kastilen (1223-1284), given the nickname of "The Wise," The Astronomer." He formed a collegium of fifty Arabic, Jewish, and Christian astronomers. This collegium brought out the so-called "Alfonsian Tables" in 1252. The saying: "If God had asked me for advice with the creation of the world, I would have made it simpler" is quoted in Gottfried Wilhelm von Leibniz's *Thoedice*, Hannover/Leipzig 1744.

Page 41-42, "Once I suggested that we assume the sacrifice of Abraham"
In the lecture of November 14, 1909, in *The Deeper Secrets in Human History* (CW 117).

Page 42, "Could I not summon a whole choir of angels..."
Matt. 26:53.

Page 43, "He who dipped his hand with me..."
John 13:26; Matt. 26:33.

Page 45, "which ripple as Moon mass..."
It is possible that "Moon water" was said and that the term "Moon mass" ("mass" was used in speaking of "cloud masses") slipped into the listeners' reports from which the content of these lectures was taken.

Page 46, "Berlin, November 21, 1911"
This lecture was given on the hundredth anniversary of the death by his own hand of the German dramatist, poet, and prose writer—the "genius's genius"—Heinrich von Kleist (1777-1811). See Joachim Maas, *Kleist, A Biography* (New York: Farrar, Strauss, and Giroux, 1983) and Philip B. Miller, ed. and trans., *An Abyss Deep Enough, Letters of Heinrich von Kleist, with a Selection of Essays and Anecdotes* (New York: Dutton, l982).

Page 47, "Cain's confrontation with Abel in the Bible..."
For other aspects of the significance of the story of Cain and Abel, see Rudolf Steiner, *The Temple Legend* (CW 93) (London: Rudolf Steiner Press, 2002) 20 lectures, Berlin, between May 23, 1904 and January 2, 1906, and *The Effects of Spiritual Development* (CW 145) (Great Barrington, MA: SteinerBooks, The Collected Works of Rudolf Steiner, 2006) 10 lectures, The Hague, March 20-29, 1913, and 1 lecture, Berlin, February 3, 1913.

Page 48, "next Thursday's public lecture..."
Lecture of November 23, 1911. In Rudolf Steiner, *Menschengeschichte im Lichte der Geistesforschung (Human History in the Light of Spiritual Research)* (GA 61) (Dornach: Rudolf Steiner Verlag, 1983) 16 lectures, Berlin, between October 19, 1911 and March 28, 1912. This volume has not been translated into English.

Page 48, "Only one who knows longing knows what I suffer."
Line from Mignon's song in Goethe's *Wilhelm Meister*.

Page 55, "I shall show this the day after tomorrow..."
Lecture of November 23, 1911. See Rudolf Steiner, *Menschengeschichte im Lichte der Geistesforschung* (GA 61) (Dornach: Rudolf Steiner Verlag, 1983).

Page 58, "the small is just like the great."
Heinrich von Kleist, letter of August 31, 1806. See Eirch Schmidt, ed., *Kleists Saemtiliche Werke* (Leipzig and Vienna, 1905), vol. 5, p. 326ff.

On November 21, at 4 p.m. in the Stimmings Inn in Potsdam, von Kleist shot Henriette Vogel and then shot himself. On the morning of his death he wrote to his friend and cousin (by marriage), Marie von Kleist: "My dear Marie, if you knew how death and love took turns crowning these last moments of my life with blossoms, those of heaven, and those of earth, surely you would be willing to let me die. I assure you, I am wholly joyous. Mornings and evenings I kneel down, something I could never do before, and I pray to God. For this my life, the most tormented of any that anyone has ever lived, I can now at last thank Him, since he makes it good through the most glorious and sensual of deaths."

Page 58, "For this spirit is one who ended his life..."
See also: Heinrich von Kleist, *Penthesilea* (Tuebingen, 1808); *Das Kaethchen von Heilbronn oder Feuerprobe* (Berlin, 1810); *Prinz Friedrich von Homburg* (Berlin, 1821).

Page 59, "*The Spiritual Guidance of the Individual and Humanity...*"
Rudolf Steiner, *The Spiritual Guidance of the Individual and of Humanity* (CW 15) (Hudson, NY: Anthroposophic Press, 1991) 3 lectures, Copenhagen, June 6-8, 1911, were afterwards compiled in written form by Steiner and published in August 1911.

Page 59, "Kleist's *Penthesilea*"
In 1806, Kleist wrote his ferocious tragedy *Penthesilea*, based on the Greek legend of the bloody battle between Achilles and Penthesilea, the Queen of the Amazons, and offered it to Goethe "on the knees of my heart." Kleist called it his most personal work: "My innermost nature is contained in it."

Page 59, "How much more there is…"
Cf. Joachim Maas, *Kleist, A Biography*, (New York: Farrar, Strauss, and Giroux, 1983) p. 142: "Kleist, a psychological visionary of the first rank, possessed a knowledge which his contemporaries had no suspicion of and which, when it was brought to their attention in *Penthesilea*, they did not understand. He had insights which today are the concern of depth psychology and which have been expressed most uncannily by Rainer Maria Rilke (1875-1926) in his *Duino Elegies*. In a very strange way, Kleist had followed Rousseau "back to nature" and with clairvoyant eye looked into the darkness of the human soul. But people of his time did not understand him."

Page 59, "the one portrayed in *Kätie of Heilbronn*"
"No sooner had *Penthesilea* seen the light of day than a counterfigure, in *Kätie of Heilbronn (or The Ordeal by Fire: A Great Historical Chivalry Play)*, made her appearance." Joachim Maas, *Kleist, A Biography*, p. 134.

Page 59, "the tragedy of *Prince of Homburg*…"
Kleist's last play, *Prince Friedrich of Homburg*, written in 1810 and published posthumously in 1821, was "a work that Nietzsche described as approaching closest among the moderns to that 'almost mystical idea,' a rebirth of tragedy." Philip B. Miller, ed., *An Abyss Deep Enough*.

Page 64, "All philosophy … arises out of wonder."
See Plato, *Theaetetus*, 155c and Aristotle, *Metaphysics*, 982b.

Page 72, "If you recall my lecture on the nature of plants."
This lecture given by Rudolf Steiner in Berlin, December 8, 1910, entitled "*Der Geist im Pflanzenreich*," *(The Spirit within the Plant Kingdom)* was published in Rudolf Steiner, *Antworten der Geisteswissenschaft auf die grossen Fragen des Daseins (The Answers of Spiritual Science to the Biggest Questions of Existence)* (GA 60) 15 lectures, Berlin, October 20, 1910-March 16, 1911.

Page 74, "as Paul did at Damascus."
Acts 9. See Rudolf Steiner, *Das Ereignis der Christus-Erscheinung in der aetherischen Welt*, (GA 118) (Dornach, Rudolf Steiner Verlag, 1984) 16 lectures, various cities, January 25-April 13, 1910. See also Rudolf Steiner, *The Reappearance of Christ in the Etheric* (selected lectures from CW 118 and other lecture cycles) (Great Barrington, MA: Anthroposophic Press, 2003) 13 lectures, various cities, 1910-1917.

Page 77, "In the lecture…"
Lecture by Rudolf Steiner in Stuttgart, November 29, 1911: "*Wie begruendet man Theosophie?*" *(How Does One Substantiate Theosophy?)* Only an incomplete transcript of the lecture exists, thus the lecture has not been published. See the lectures given in Berlin on October 31 and November 7, 1912, published in *Ergebnisse der Geistesforschung (Results of Spiritual Research)* (GA 62) 14 lectures, Berlin, October 31, 1912-April 10, 1913. The story of the little boy and the purchase of the rolls was used as a starting point in a lecture cycle given in Hanover: *Die Welt der Sinne und die Welt des Geistes (The World of Senses and the World of the Spirit)* (GA 134) 6 lectures, Hanover, December 27, 1911-January 1, 1912.

Page 78, "for a fundamental understanding of what is in the Gospel of Saint Mark…"
See Rudolf Steiner, *The Gospel of Saint Mark* (CW 139) (Hudson, NY: Anthroposophic Press, 1986) 10 lectures, Basel, September 15-24, 1912.

RUDOLF STEINER'S COLLECTED WORKS

The German Edition of Rudolf Steiner's Collected Works (the Gesamtausgabe [GA] published by Rudolf Steiner Verlag, Dornach, Switzerland) presently runs to over 354 titles, organized either by type of work (written or spoken), chronology, audience (public or other), or subject (education, art, etc.). For ease of comparison, the Collected Works in English [CW] follows the German organization exactly. A complete listing of the CWs follows with literal translations of the German titles. Other than in the case of the books published in his lifetime, titles were rarely given by Rudolf Steiner himself, and were often provided by the editors of the German editions. The titles in English are not necessarily the same as the German; and, indeed, over the past seventy-five years have frequently been different, with the same book sometimes appearing under different titles.

For ease of identification and to avoid confusion, we suggest that readers looking for a title should do so by CW number. Because the work of creating the Collected Works of Rudolf Steiner is an ongoing process, with new titles being published every year, we have not indicated in this listing which books are presently available. To find out what titles in the Collected Works are currently in print, please check our website at www.steinerbooks.org, or write to SteinerBooks 610 Main Street, Great Barrington, MA 01230:

Written Work

CW 1	Goethe: Natural-Scientific Writings, Introduction, with Footnotes and Explanations in the text by Rudolf Steiner
CW 2	Outlines of an Epistemology of the Goethean World View, with Special Consideration of Schiller
CW 3	Truth and Science
CW 4	The Philosophy of Freedom
CW 4a	Documents to "The Philosophy of Freedom"
CW 5	Friedrich Nietzsche, A Fighter against His Own Time
CW 6	Goethe's Worldview
CW 6a	Now in CW 30
CW 7	Mysticism at the Dawn of Modern Spiritual Life and Its Relationship with Modern Worldviews
CW 8	Christianity as Mystical Fact and the Mysteries of Antiquity
CW 9	Theosophy: An Introduction into Supersensible World Knowledge and Human Purpose
CW 10	How Does One Attain Knowledge of Higher Worlds?
CW 11	From the Akasha-Chronicle
CW 12	Levels of Higher Knowledge

CW 13	Occult Science in Outline
CW 14	Four Mystery Dramas
CW 15	The Spiritual Guidance of the Individual and Humanity
CW 16	A Way to Human Self-Knowledge: Eight Meditations
CW 17	The Threshold of the Spiritual World. Aphoristic Comments
CW 18	The Riddles of Philosophy in Their History, Presented as an Outline
CW 19	Contained in CW 24
CW 20	The Riddles of the Human Being: Articulated and Unarticulated in the Thinking, Views and Opinions of a Series of German and Austrian Personalities
CW 21	The Riddles of the Soul
CW 22	Goethe's Spiritual Nature And Its Revelation In "Faust" and through the "Fairy Tale of the Snake and the Lily"
CW 23	The Central Points of the Social Question in the Necessities of Life in the Present and the Future
CW 24	Essays Concerning the Threefold Division of the Social Organism and the Period 1915-1921
CW 25	Cosmology, Religion and Philosophy
CW 26	Anthroposophical Leading Thoughts
CW 27	Fundamentals for Expansion of the Art of Healing according to Spiritual-Scientific Insights
CW 28	The Course of My Life
CW 29	Collected Essays on Dramaturgy, 1889-1900
CW 30	Methodical Foundations of Anthroposophy: Collected Essays on Philosophy, Natural Science, Aesthetics and Psychology, 1884-1901
CW 31	Collected Essays on Culture and Current Events, 1887-1901
CW 32	Collected Essays on Literature, 1884-1902
CW 33	Biographies and Biographical Sketches, 1894-1905
CW 34	Lucifer-Gnosis: Foundational Essays on Anthroposophy and Reports from the Periodicals "Lucifer" and "Lucifer-Gnosis," 1903-1908
CW 35	Philosophy and Anthroposophy: Collected Essays, 1904-1923
CW 36	The Goetheanum-Idea in the Middle of the Cultural Crisis of the Present: Collected Essays from the Periodical "Das Goetheanum," 1921-1925
CW 37	Now in CWs 260a and 251
CW 38	Letters, Vol. 1: 1881-1890
CW 39	Letters, Vol. 2: 1890-1925
CW 40	Truth-Wrought Words
CW 40a	Sayings, Poems and Mantras; Supplementary Volume
CW 42	Now in CWs 264-266

CW 43   Stage Adaptations
CW 44   On the Four Mystery Dramas. Sketches, Fragments and Paralipomena on the Four Mystery Dramas
CW 45   Anthroposophy: A Fragment from the Year 1910

Public Lectures

CW 51   On Philosophy, History and Literature
CW 52   Spiritual Teachings Concerning the Soul and Observation of the World
CW 53   The Origin and Goal of the Human Being
CW 54   The Riddles of the World and Anthroposophy
CW 55   Knowledge of the Supersensible in Our Times and Its Meaning for Life Today
CW 56   Knowledge of the Soul and of the Spirit
CW 57   Where and How Does One Find the Spirit?
CW 58   The Metamorphoses of the Soul Life. Paths of Soul Experiences: Part One
CW 59   The Metamorphoses of the Soul Life. Paths of Soul Experiences: Part Two
CW 60   The Answers of Spiritual Science to the Biggest Questions of Existence
CW 61   Human History in the Light of Spiritual Research
CW 62   Results of Spiritual Research
CW 63   Spiritual Science as a Treasure for Life
CW 64   Out of Destiny-Burdened Times
CW 65   Out of Central European Spiritual Life
CW 66   Spirit and Matter, Life and Death
CW 67   The Eternal in the Human Soul. Immortality and Freedom
CW 68   Public lectures in various cities, 1906-1918
CW 69   Public lectures in various cities, 1906-1918
CW 70   Public lectures in various cities, 1906-1918
CW 71   Public lectures in various cities, 1906-1918
CW 72   Freedom – Immortality – Social Life
CW 73   The Supplementing of the Modern Sciences through Anthroposophy
CW 73a   Specialized Fields of Knowledge and Anthroposophy
CW 74   The Philosophy of Thomas Aquinas
CW 75   Public lectures in various cities, 1906-1918
CW 76   The Fructifying Effect of Anthroposophy on Specialized Fields
CW 77a   The Task of Anthroposophy in Relation to Science and Life: The Darmstadt College Course
CW 77b   Art and Anthroposophy. The Goetheanum-Impulse

CW 78   Anthroposophy, Its Roots of Knowledge and Fruits for Life
CW 79   The Reality of the Higher Worlds
CW 80   Public lectures in various cities, 1922
CW 81   Renewal-Impulses for Culture and Science–Berlin College Course
CW 82   So that the Human Being Can Become a Complete Human Being
CW 83   Western and Eastern World-Contrast. Paths to Understanding It through Anthroposophy
CW 84   What Did the Goetheanum Intend and What Should Anthroposophy Do?

Lectures to the Members of the Anthroposophical Society

CW 88   Concerning the Astral World and Devachan
CW 89   Consciousness–Life–Form. Fundamental Principles of a Spiritual-Scientific Cosmology
CW 90   Participant Notes from the Lectures during the Years 1903-1905
CW 91   Participant Notes from the Lectures during the Years 1903-1905
CW 92   The Occult Truths of Ancient Myths and Sagas
CW 93   The Temple Legend and the Golden Legend
CW 93a Fundamentals of Esotericism
CW 94   Cosmogony. Popular Occultism. The Gospel of John. The Theosophy in the Gospel of John
CW 95   At the Gates of Theosophy
CW 96   Origin-Impulses of Spiritual Science. Christian Esotericism in the Light of New Spirit-Knowledge
CW 97   The Christian Mystery
CW 98   Nature Beings and Spirit Beings – Their Effects in Our Visible World
CW 99   The Theosophy of the Rosicrucians
CW 100 Human Development and Christ-Knowledge
CW 101 Myths and Legends. Occult Signs and Symbols
CW 102 The Working into Human Beings by Spiritual Beings
CW 103 The Gospel of John
CW 104 The Apocalypse of John
CW 104a From the Picture-Script of the Apocalypse of John
CW 105 Universe, Earth, the Human Being: Their Being and Development, as well as Their Reflection in the Connection between Egyptian Mythology and Modern Culture
CW 106 Egyptian Myths and Mysteries in Relation to the Active Spiritual Forces of the Present
CW 107 Spiritual-Scientific Knowledge of the Human Being
CW 108 Answering the Questions of Life and the World through Anthroposophy

Rudolf Steiner's Collected Works * 89

CW 109	The Principle of Spiritual Economy in Connection with the Question of Reincarnation. An Aspect of the Spiritual Guidance of Humanity
CW 110	The Spiritual Hierarchies and Their Reflection in the Physical World. Zodiac, Planets and Cosmos
CW 111	Contained in 109
CW 112	The Gospel of John in Relation to the Three Other Gospels, Especially the Gospel of Luke
CW 113	The Orient in the Light of the Occident. The Children of Lucifer and the Brothers of Christ
CW 114	The Gospel of Luke
CW 115	Anthroposophy – Psychosophy – Pneumatosophy
CW 116	The Christ-Impulse and the Development of "I"- Consciousness
CW 117	The Deeper Secrets of the Development of Humanity in Light of the Gospels
CW 118	The Event of the Christ-Appearance in the Etheric World
CW 119	Macrocosm and Microcosm. The Large World and the Small World. Soul-Questions, Life-Questions, Spirit-Questions
CW 120	The Revelation of Karma
CW 121	The Mission of Individual Folk-Souls in Connection with Germanic-Nordic Mythology
CW 122	The Secrets of the Biblical Creation-Story. The Six-Day Work in the First Book of Moses
CW 123	The Gospel of Matthew
CW 124	Excursus in the Area of the Gospel of Mark
CW 125	Paths and Goals of the Spiritual Human Being. Life Questions in the Light of Spiritual Science
CW 126	Occult History. Esoteric Observations of the Karmic Relationships of Personalities and Events of World History
CW 127	The Mission of the New Spiritual Revelation. The Christ-Event as the Middle-Point of Earth Evolution
CW 128	An Occult Physiology
CW 129	Wonders of the World, Trials of the Soul, and Revelations of the Spirit
CW 130	Esoteric Christianity and the Spiritual Guidance of Humanity
CW 131	From Jesus to Christ
CW 132	Evolution from the View Point of the Truth
CW 133	The Earthly and the Cosmic Human Being
CW 134	The World of the Senses and the World of the Spirit
CW 135	Reincarnation and Karma and their Meaning for the Culture of the Present
CW 136	The Spiritual Beings in Celestial Bodies and the Realms of Nature

CW 137	The Human Being in the Light of Occultism, Theosophy and Philosophy
CW 138	On Initiation. On Eternity and the Passing Moment. On the Light of the Spirit and the Darkness of Life
CW 139	The Gospel of Mark
CW 140	Occult Investigation into the Life between Death and New Birth. The Living Interaction between Life and Death
CW 141	Life between Death and New Birth in Relationship to Cosmic Facts
CW 142	The Bhagavad Gita and the Letters of Paul
CW 143	Experiences of the Supersensible. Three Paths of the Soul to Christ
CW 144	The Mysteries of the East and of Christianity
CW 145	What Significance Does Occult Development of the Human Being Have for His Sheaths–Physical Body, Etheric Body, Astral Body, and Self?
CW 146	The Occult Foundations of the Bhagavad Gita
CW 147	The Secrets of the Threshold
CW 148	Out of Research in the Akasha: The Fifth Gospel
CW 149	Christ and the Spiritual World. Concerning the Search for the Holy Grail
CW 150	The World of the Spirit and Its Extension into Physical Existence; The Influence of the Dead in the World of the Living
CW 151	Human Thought and Cosmic Thought
CW 152	Preliminary Stages to the Mystery of Golgotha
CW 153	The Inner Being of the Human Being and Life Between Death and New Birth
CW 154	How does One Gain an Understanding of the Spiritual World? The Flowing in of Spiritual Impulses from out of the World of the Deceased
CW 155	Christ and the Human Soul. Concerning the Meaning of Life. Theosophical Morality. Anthroposophy and Christianity
CW 156	Occult Reading and Occult Hearing
CW 157	Human Destinies and the Destiny of Peoples
CW 157a	The Formation of Destiny and the Life after Death
CW 158	The Connection Between the Human Being and the Elemental World. Kalevala – Olaf Asteson – The Russian People – The World as the Result of the Influences of Equilibrium
CW 159	The Mystery of Death. The Nature and Significance of Middle Europe and the European Folk Spirits
CW 160	In CW 159
CW 161	Paths of Spiritual Knowledge and the Renewal of the Artistic Worldview
CW 162	Questions of Art and Life in Light of Spiritual Science

CW 163	Coincidence, Necessity and Providence. Imaginative Knowledge and the Processes after Death
CW 164	The Value of Thinking for a Knowledge That Satisfies the Human Being. The Relationship of Spiritual Science to Natural Science
CW 165	The Spiritual Unification of Humanity through the Christ-Impulse
CW 166	Necessity and Freedom in the Events of the World and in Human Action
CW 167	The Present and the Past in the Human Spirit
CW 168	The Connection between the Living and the Dead
CW 169	World-being and Selfhood
CW 170	The Riddle of the Human Being. The Spiritual Background of Human History. Cosmic and Human History, Vol. 1
CW 171	Inner Development-Impulses of Humanity. Goethe and the Crisis of the 19th Century. Cosmic and Human History, Vol. 2
CW 172	The Karma of the Vocation of the Human Being in Connection with Goethe's Life. Cosmic and Human History, Vol. 3
CW 173	Contemporary-Historical Considerations: The Karma of Untruthfulness, Part One. Cosmic and Human History, Vol. 4
CW 174	Contemporary-Historical Considerations: The Karma of Untruthfulness, Part Two. Cosmic and Human History, Vol. 5
CW 174a	Middle Europe between East and West. Cosmic and Human History, Vol. 6
CW 174b	The Spiritual Background of the First World War. Cosmic and Human History, Vol. 7
CW 175	Building Stones for an Understanding of the Mystery of Golgotha. Cosmic and Human Metamorphoses
CW 176	Truths of Evolution of the Individual and Humanity. The Karma of Materialism
CW 177	The Spiritual Background of the Outer World. The Fall of the Spirits of Darkness. Spiritual Beings and Their Effects, Vol. 1
CW 178	Individual Spiritual Beings and their Influence in the Soul of the Human Being. Spiritual Beings and their Effects, Vol. 2
CW 179	Spiritual Beings and Their Effects. Historical Necessity and Freedom. The Influences on Destiny from out of the World of the Dead. Spiritual Beings and Their Effects, Vol. 3
CW 180	Mystery Truths and Christmas Impulses. Ancient Myths and their Meaning. Spiritual Beings and Their Effects, Vol. 4
CW 181	Earthly Death and Cosmic Life. Anthroposophical Gifts for Life. Necessities of Consciousness for the Present and the Future.
CW 182	Death as Transformation of Life
CW 183	The Science of the Development of the Human Being
CW 184	The Polarity of Duration and Development in Human Life. The Cosmic Pre-History of Humanity

CW 185	Historical Symptomology
CW 185a	Historical-Developmental Foundations for Forming a Social Judgment
CW 186	The Fundamental Social Demands of Our Time–In Changed Situations
CW 187	How Can Humanity Find the Christ Again? The Threefold Shadow-Existence of our Time and the New Christ-Light
CW 188	Goetheanism, a Transformation-Impulse and Resurrection-Thought. Science of the Human Being and Science of Sociology
CW 189	The Social Question as a Question of Consciousness. The Spiritual Background of the Social Question, Vol. 1
CW 190	Impulses of the Past and the Future in Social Occurrences. The Spiritual Background of the Social Question, Vol. 2
CW 191	Social Understanding from Spiritual-Scientific Cognition. The Spiritual Background of the Social Question, Vol. 3
CW 192	Spiritual-Scientific Treatment of Social and Pedagogical Questions
CW 193	The Inner Aspect of the Social Riddle. Luciferic Past and Ahrimanic Future
CW 194	The Mission of Michael. The Revelation of the Actual Mysteries of the Human Being
CW 195	Cosmic New Year and the New Year Idea
CW 196	Spiritual and Social Transformations in the Development of Humanity
CW 197	Polarities in the Development of Humanity: West and East Materialism and Mysticism Knowledge and Belief
CW 198	Healing Factors for the Social Organism
CW 199	Spiritual Science as Knowledge of the Foundational Impulses of Social Formation
CW 200	The New Spirituality and the Christ-Experience of the 20th Century
CW 201	The Correspondences Between Microcosm and Macrocosm. The Human Being – A Hieroglyph of the Universe. The Human Being in Relationship with the Cosmos: 1
CW 202	The Bridge between the World-Spirituality and the Physical Aspect of the Human Being. The Search for the New Isis, the Divine Sophia. The Human Being in Relationship with the Cosmos: 2
CW 203	The Responsibility of Human Beings for the Development of the World through their Spiritual Connection with the Planet Earth and the World of the Stars. The Human Being in Relationship with the Cosmos: 3
CW 204	Perspectives of the Development of Humanity. The Materialistic Knowledge-Impulse and the Task of Anthroposophy. The Human Being in Relationship with the Cosmos: 4

CW 205	Human Development, World-Soul, and World-Spirit. Part One: The Human Being as a Being of Body and Soul in Relationship to the World. The Human Being in Relationship with the Cosmos: 5
CW 206	Human Development, World-Soul, and World-Spirit. Part Two: The Human Being as a Spiritual Being in the Process of Historical Development. The Human Being in Relationship with the Cosmos: 6
CW 207	Anthroposophy as Cosmosophy. Part One: Characteristic Features of the Human Being in the Earthly and the Cosmic Realms. The Human Being in Relationship with the Cosmos: 7
CW 208	Anthroposophy as Cosmosophy. Part Two: The Forming of the Human Being as the Result of Cosmic Influence. The Human Being in Relationship with the Cosmos: 8
CW 209	Nordic and Central European Spiritual Impulses. The Festival of the Appearance of Christ. The Human Being in Relationship with the Cosmos: 9
CW 210	Old and New Methods of Initiation. Drama and Poetry in the Change of Consciousness in the Modern Age
CW 211	The Sun Mystery and the Mystery of Death and Resurrection. Exoteric and Esoteric Christianity
CW 212	Human Soul Life and Spiritual Striving in Connection with World and Earth Development
CW 213	Human Questions and World Answers
CW 214	The Mystery of the Trinity: The Human Being in Relationship to the Spiritual World in the Course of Time
CW 215	Philosophy, Cosmology, and Religion in Anthroposophy
CW 216	The Fundamental Impulses of the World-Historical Development of Humanity
CW 217	Spiritually Active Forces in the Coexistence of the Older and Younger Generations. Pedagogical Course for Youth
CW 217a	Youth's Cognitive Task
CW 218	Spiritual Connections in the Forming of the Human Organism
CW 219	The Relationship of the World of the Stars to the Human Being, and of the Human Being to the World of the Stars. The Spiritual Communion of Humanity
CW 220	Living Knowledge of Nature. Intellectual Fall and Spiritual Redemption
CW 221	Earth-Knowing and Heaven-Insight
CW 222	The Imparting of Impulses to World-Historical Events through Spiritual Powers
CW 223	The Cycle of the Year as Breathing Process of the Earth and the Four Great Festival-Seasons. Anthroposophy and Human Heart (Gemüt)

CW 224	The Human Soul and its Connection with Divine-Spiritual Individualities. The Internalization of the Festivals of the Year
CW 225	Three Perspectives of Anthroposophy. Cultural Phenomena observed from a Spiritual-Scientific Perspective
CW 226	Human Being, Human Destiny, and World Development
CW 227	Initiation-Knowledge
CW 228	Science of Initiation and Knowledge of the Stars. The Human Being in the Past, the Present, and the Future from the Viewpoint of the Development of Consciousness
CW 229	The Experiencing of the Course of the Year in Four Cosmic Imaginations
CW 230	The Human Being as Harmony of the Creative, Building, and Formative World-Word
CW 231	The Supersensible Human Being, Understood Anthroposophically
CW 232	The Forming of the Mysteries
CW 233	World History Illuminated by Anthroposophy and as the Foundation for Knowledge of the Human Spirit
CW 233a	Mystery Sites of the Middle Ages: Rosicrucianism and the Modern Initiation-Principle. The Festival of Easter as Part of the History of the Mysteries of Humanity
CW 234	Anthroposophy. A Summary after 21 Years
CW 235	Esoteric Observations of Karmic Relationships in 6 Volumes, Vol. 1
CW 236	Esoteric Observations of Karmic Relationships in 6 Volumes, Vol. 2
CW 237	Esoteric Observations of Karmic Relationships in 6 Volumes, Vol. 3: The Karmic Relationships of the Anthroposophical Movement
CW 238	Esoteric Observations of Karmic Relationships in 6 Volumes, Vol. 4: The Spiritual Life of the Present in Relationship to the Anthroposophical Movement
CW 239	Esoteric Observations of Karmic Relationships in 6 Volumes, Vol. 5
CW 240	Esoteric Observations of Karmic Relationships in 6 Volumes, Vol. 6
CW 243	The Consciousness of the Initiate
CW 245	Instructions for an Esoteric Schooling
CW 250	The Building-Up of the Anthroposophical Society. From the Beginning to the Outbreak of the First World War
CW 251	The History of the Goetheanum Building-Association
CW 252	Life in the Anthroposophical Society from the First World War to the Burning of the First Goetheanum
CW 253	The Problems of Living Together in the Anthroposophical Society. On the Dornach Crisis of 1915. With Highlights on Swedenborg's Clairvoyance, the Views of Freudian Psychoanalysts, and the Concept of Love in Relation to Mysticism

CW 254	The Occult Movement in the 19th Century and Its Relationship to World Culture. Significant Points from the Exoteric Cultural Life around the Middle of the 19th Century
CW 255	Rudolf Steiner during the First World War
CW 255a	Anthroposophy and the Reformation of Society. On the History of the Threefold Movement
CW 255b	Anthroposophy and Its Opponents, 1919-1921
CW 256	How Can the Anthroposophical Movement Be Financed?
CW 256a	Futurum, Inc. / International Laboratories, Inc.
CW 256b	The Coming Day, Inc.
CW 257	Anthroposophical Community-Building
CW 258	The History of and Conditions for the Anthroposophical Movement in Relationship to the Anthroposophical Society. A Stimulus to Self-Contemplation
CW 259	The Year of Destiny 1923 in the History of the Anthroposophical Society. From the Burning of the Goetheanum to the Christmas Conference
CW 260	The Christmas Conference for the Founding of the General Anthroposophical Society
CW 260a	The Constitution of the General Anthroposophical Society and the School for Spiritual Science. The Rebuilding of the Goetheanum
CW 261	Our Dead. Addresses, Words of Remembrance, and Meditative Verses, 1906-1924
CW 262	Rudolf Steiner and Marie Steiner-von Sivers: Correspondence and Documents, 1901-1925
CW 263/1	Rudolf Steiner and Edith Maryon: Correspondence: Letters, Verses, Sketches, 1912-1924
CW 264	On the History and the Contents of the First Section of the Esoteric School from 1904 to 1914. Letters, Newsletters, Documents, Lectures
CW 265	On the History and Out of the Contents of the Ritual-Knowledge Section of the Esoteric School from 1904 to 1914. Documents, and Lectures from the Years 1906 to 1914, as well as on New Approaches to Ritual-Knowledge Work in the Years 1921-1924
CW 266/1	From the Contents of the Esoteric Lessons. Volume 1: 1904-1909. Notes from Memory of Participants. Meditation texts from the notes of Rudolf Steiner
CW 266/2	From the Contents of the Esoteric Lessons. Volume 2: 1910-1912. Notes from Memory of Participants
CW 266/3	From the Contents of the Esoteric Lessons. Volume 3: 1913, 1914 and 1920-1923. Notes from Memory of Participants. Meditation texts from the notes of Rudolf Steiner

CW 267	Soul-Exercises: Vol. 1: Exercises with Word and Image Meditations for the Methodological Development of Higher Powers of Knowledge, 1904-1924
CW 268	Soul-Exercises: Vol. 2: Mantric Verses, 1903-1925
CW 269	Ritual Texts for the Celebration of the Free Christian Religious Instruction. The Collected Verses for Teachers and Students of the Waldorf School
CW 270	Esoteric Instructions for the First Class of the School for Spiritual Science at the Goetheanum 1924, 4 Volumes
CW 271	Art and Knowledge of Art. Foundations of a New Aesthetic
CW 272	Spiritual-Scientific Commentary on Goethe's "Faust" in Two Volumes. Vol. 1: Faust, the Striving Human Being
CW 273	Spiritual-Scientific Commentary on Goethe's "Faust" in Two Volumes. Vol. 2: The Faust-Problem
CW 274	Addresses for the Christmas Plays from the Old Folk Traditions
CW 275	Art in the Light of Mystery-Wisdom
CW 276	The Artistic in Its Mission in the World. The Genius of Language. The World of the Self-Revealing Radiant Appearances – Anthroposophy and Art. Anthroposophy and Poetry
CW 277	Eurythmy. The Revelation of the Speaking Soul
CW 277a	The Origin and Development of Eurythmy
CW 278	Eurythmy as Visible Song
CW 279	Eurythmy as Visible Speech
CW 280	The Method and Nature of Speech Formation
CW 281	The Art of Recitation and Declamation
CW 282	Speech Formation and Dramatic Art
CW 283	The Nature of Things Musical and the Experience of Tone in the Human Being
CW 284/285	Images of Occult Seals and Pillars. The Munich Congress of Whitsun 1907 and Its Consequences
CW 286	Paths to a New Style of Architecture. "And the Building Becomes Human"
CW 287	The Building at Dornach as a Symbol of Historical Becoming and an Artistic Transformation Impulse
CW 288	Style-Forms in the Living Organic
CW 289	The Building-Idea of the Goetheanum: Lectures with Slides from the Years 1920-1921
CW 290	The Building-Idea of the Goetheanum: Lectures with Slides from the Years 1920-1921
CW 291	The Nature of Colors
CW 291a	Knowledge of Colors. Supplementary Volume to "The Nature of Colors"
CW 292	Art History as Image of Inner Spiritual Impulses

CW 293	General Knowledge of the Human Being as the Foundation of Pedagogy
CW 294	The Art of Education, Methodology and Didactics
CW 295	The Art of Education: Seminar Discussions and Lectures on Lesson Planning
CW 296	The Question of Education as a Social Question
CW 297	The Idea and Practice of the Waldorf School
CW 297a	Education for Life: Self-Education and the Practice of Pedagogy
CW 298	Rudolf Steiner in the Waldorf School
CW 299	Spiritual-Scientific Observations on Speech
CW 300a	Conferences with the Teachers of the Free Waldorf School in Stuttgart, 1919 to 1924, in 3 Volumes, Vol. 1
CW 300b	Conferences with the Teachers of the Free Waldorf School in Stuttgart, 1919 to 1924, in 3 Volumes, Vol. 2
CW 300c	Conferences with the Teachers of the Free Waldorf School in Stuttgart, 1919 to 1924, in 3 Volumes, Vol. 3
CW 301	The Renewal of the Pedagogical-Didactical Art through Spiritual Science
CW 302	Knowledge of the Human Being and the Forming of Class Lessons
CW 302a	Education and Teaching out of a Knowledge of the Human Being
CW 303	The Healthy Development of the Human Being
CW 304	Methods of Education and Teaching Based on Anthroposophy
CW 304a	Anthroposophical Knowledge of the Human Being and Pedagogy
CW 305	The Soul-Spiritual Foundational Forces of the Art of Education. Spiritual Values in Education and Social Life
CW 306	Pedagogical Praxis from the Viewpoint of a Spiritual-Scientific Knowledge of the Human Being. The Education of the Child and Young Human Beings
CW 307	The Spiritual Life of the Present and Education
CW 308	The Method of Teaching and the Life-Requirements for Teaching
CW 309	Anthroposophical Pedagogy and Its Prerequisites
CW 310	The Pedagogical Value of a Knowledge of the Human Being and the Cultural Value of Pedagogy
CW 311	The Art of Education Out of an Understanding of the Being of Humanity
CW 312	Spiritual Science and Medicine
CW 313	Spiritual-Scientific Viewpoints on Therapy
CW 314	Physiology and Therapy Based on Spiritual Science
CW 315	Curative Eurythmy
CW 316	Meditative Observations and Instructions for a Deepening of the Art of Healing
CW 317	The Curative Education Course
CW 318	The Working Together of Doctors and Pastors

CW 319   Anthroposophical Knowledge of the Human Being and Medicine
CW 320   Spiritual-Scientific Impulses for the Development of Physics 1: The First Natural-Scientific Course: Light, Color, Tone, Mass, Electricity, Magnetism
CW 321   Spiritual-Scientific Impulses for the Development of Physics 2: The Second Natural-Scientific Course: Warmth at the Border of Positive and Negative Materiality
CW 322   The Borders of the Knowledge of Nature
CW 323   The Relationship of the various Natural-Scientific Fields to Astronomy
CW 324   Nature Observation, Mathematics, and Scientific Experimentation and Results from the Viewpoint of Anthroposophy
CW 324a   The Fourth Dimension in Mathematics and Reality
CW 325   Natural Science and the World-Historical Development of Humanity since Ancient Times
CW 326   The Moment of the Coming Into Being of Natural Science in World History and Its Development Since Then
CW 327   Spiritual-Scientific Foundations for Success in Farming. The Agricultural Course
CW 328   The Social Question
CW 329   The Liberation of the Human Being as the Foundation for a New Social Form
CW 330   The Renewal of the Social Organism
CW 331   Work-Council and Socialization
CW 332   The Alliance for Threefolding and the Total Reform of Society. The Council on Culture and the Liberation of the Spiritual Life
CW 332a   The Social Future
CW 333   Freedom of Thought and Social Forces
CW 334   From the Unified State to the Threefold Social Organism
CW 335   The Crisis of the Present and the Path to Healthy Thinking
CW 336   The Great Questions of the Times and Anthroposophical Spiritual Knowledge
CW 337a   Social Ideas, Social Reality, Social Practice, Vol. 1: Question-and- Answer Evenings and Study Evenings of the Alliance for the Threefold Social Organism in Stuttgart, 1919-1920
CW 337b   Social Ideas, Social Realities, Social Practice, Vol. 2: Discussion Evenings of the Swiss Alliance for the Threefold Social Organism
CW 338   How Does One Work on Behalf of the Impulse for the Threefold Social Organism?
CW 339   Anthroposophy, Threefold Social Organism, and the Art of Public Speaking
CW 340   The National-Economics Course. The Tasks of a New Science of Economics, Volume 1

CW 341   The National-Economics Seminar. The Tasks of a New Science of Economics, Volume 2
CW 342   Lectures and Courses on Christian Religious Work, Vol. 1: Anthroposophical Foundations for a Renewed Christian Religious Working
CW 343   Lectures and Courses on Christian Religious Work, Vol. 2: Spiritual Knowledge – Religious Feeling – Cultic Doing
CW 344   Lectures and Courses on Christian Religious Work, Vol. 3: Lectures at the Founding of the Christian Community
CW 345   Lectures and Courses on Christian Religious Work, Vol. 4: Concerning the Nature of the Working Word
CW 346   Lectures and Courses on Christian Religious Work, Vol. 5: The Apocalypse and the Working of the Priest
CW 347   The Knowledge of the Nature of the Human Being According to Body, Soul and Spirit. On Earlier Conditions of the Earth
CW 348   On Health and Illness. Foundations of a Spiritual-Scientific Doctrine of the Senses
CW 349   On the Life of Human Being and of the Earth. On the Nature of Christianity
CW 350   Rhythms in the Cosmos and in the Human Being. How Does One Come To See the Spiritual World?
CW 351   The Human Being and the World. The Influence of the Spirit in Nature. On the Nature of Bees
CW 352   Nature and the Human Being Observed Spiritual-Scientifically
CW 353   The History of Humanity and the World-Views of the Folk Cultures
CW 354   The Creation of the World and the Human Being. Life on Earth and the Influence of the Stars

SIGNIFICANT EVENTS IN THE LIFE OF RUDOLF STEINER

1829: June 23: birth of Johann Steiner (1829-1910)—Rudolf Steiner's father—in Geras, Lower Austria.

1834: May 8: birth of Franciska Blie (1834-1918)—Rudolf Steiner's mother—in Horn, Lower Austria. "My father and mother were both children of the glorious Lower Austrian forest district north of the Danube."

1860: May 16: marriage of Johann Steiner and Franciska Blie.

1861: February 25: birth of *Rudolf Joseph Lorenz Steiner* in Kraljevec, Croatia, near the border with Hungary, where Johann Steiner works as a telegrapher for the South Austria Railroad. Rudolf Steiner is baptized two days later, February 27, the date usually given as his birthday.

1862: Summer: the family moves to Mödling, Lower Austria.

1863: The family moves to Pottschach, Lower Austria, near the Styrian border, where Johann Steiner becomes stationmaster. "The view stretched to the mountains...majestic peaks in the distance and the sweet charm of nature in the immediate surroundings."

1864: November 15: birth of Rudolf Steiner's sister, Leopoldine (d. November 1, 1927). She will become a seamstress and live with her parents for the rest of her life.

1866: July 28: birth of Rudolf Steiner's deaf-mute brother, Gustav (d. May 1, 1941).

1867: Rudolf Steiner enters the village school. Following a disagreement between his father and the schoolmaster, whose wife falsely accused the boy of causing a commotion, Rudolf Steiner is taken out of school and taught at home.

1868: A critical experience. Unknown to the family, an aunt dies in a distant town. Sitting in the station waiting room, Rudolf Steiner sees her "form," which speaks to him, asking for help. "Beginning with this experience, a new soul life began in the boy, one in which not only the outer trees and mountains spoke to him, but also the worlds that lay behind them. From this moment on, the boy began to live with the spirits of nature...."

1869: The family moves to the peaceful, rural village of Neudorfl, near Wiener-Neustadt in present-day Hungary. Rudolf Steiner attends the village school. Because of the "unorthodoxy" of his writing and spelling, he has to do "extra lessons."

1870: Through a book lent to him by his tutor, he discovers geometry: "To grasp something purely in the spirit brought me inner happiness. I know that I first learned happiness through geometry." The same tutor allows him to draw, while other students still struggle with their reading and writing. "An artistic element" thus enters his education.

1871: Though his parents are not religious, Rudolf Steiner becomes a "church child," a favorite of the priest, who was "an exceptional character." "Up to the age of ten or eleven, among those I came to know, he was far and away the most significant." Among other things, he introduces Steiner to Copernican, heliocentric cosmology. As an altar boy, Rudolf Steiner serves at Masses, funerals, and Corpus Christi processions. At year's end, after an incident in which he escapes a thrashing, his father forbids him to go to church.

1872: Rudolf Steiner transfers to grammar school in Wiener-Neustadt, a five-mile walk from home, which must be done in all weathers.

1873-75: Through his teachers and on his own, Rudolf Steiner has many wonderful experiences with science and mathematics. Outside school, he teaches himself analytic geometry, trigonometry, differential equations, and calculus.

1876: Rudolf Steiner begins tutoring other students. He learns bookbinding from his father. He also teaches himself stenography.

1877: Rudolf Steiner discovers Kant's *Critique of Pure Reason*, which he reads and rereads. He also discovers and reads von Rotteck's *World History*.

1878: He studies extensively in contemporary psychology and philosophy.

1879: Rudolf Steiner graduates from high school with honors. His father is transferred to Inzersdorf, near Vienna. He uses his first visit to Vienna "to purchase a great number of philosophy books"—Kant, Fichte, Schelling, and Hegel, as well as numerous histories of philosophy. His aim: to find a path from the "I" to nature.

October 1879-1883: Rudolf Steiner attends the Technical College in Vienna—to study mathematics, chemistry, physics, mineralogy, botany, zoology, biology, geology, and mechanics—with a scholarship. He also attends lectures in history and literature, while avidly reading philosophy on his own. His two favorite professors are Karl Julius Schröer (German language and literature) and Edmund Reitlinger (physics). He also audits lectures by Robert Zimmerman on aesthetics and Franz Brentano on philosophy. During this year he begins his friendship with Moritz Zitter (1861-1921), who will help support him financially when he is in Berlin.

1880: Rudolf Steiner attends lectures on Schiller and Goethe by Karl Julius Schröer, who becomes his mentor. Also "through a remarkable combination of circumstances," he meets Felix Koguzki, an "herb gatherer" and healer, who could "see deeply into the secrets of nature." Rudolf Steiner will meet and study with this "emissary of the Master" throughout his time in Vienna.

1881: January: "... I didn't sleep a wink. I was busy with philosophical problems until about 12:30 a.m. Then, finally, I threw myself down on my couch. All my striving during the previous year had been to research whether the following statement by Schelling was true or not: *Within everyone dwells a secret, marvelous capacity to draw back from the stream of time—out of the self clothed in all that comes to us from outside—into our innermost being and there, in the immutable form of the Eternal, to look into ourselves.* I believe, and I am still quite certain of it, that I discovered this capacity in myself; I had long had an inkling of it. Now the whole of idealist philosophy stood before me in modified form. What's a sleepless night compared to that!"

Rudolf Steiner begins communicating with leading thinkers of the day, who send him books in return, which he reads eagerly.

July: "I am not one of those who dives into the day like an animal in human form. I pursue a quite specific goal, an idealistic aim—knowledge of the truth! This cannot be done offhandedly. It requires the greatest striving in the world, free of all egotism, and equally of all resignation."

August: Steiner puts down on paper for the first time thoughts for a "Philosophy of Freedom." "The striving for the absolute: this human yearning is freedom." He also seeks to outline a "peasant philosophy," describing what the worldview of a "peasant"—one who lives close to the earth and the old ways—really is.

1881-1882: Felix Koguzki, the herb gatherer, reveals himself to be the envoy of another, higher initiatory personality, who instructs Rudolf Steiner to penetrate Fichte's philosophy and to master modern scientific thinking as a preparation for right entry into the spirit. This "Master" also teaches him the double (evolutionary and involutionary) nature of time.

1882: Through the offices of Karl Julius Schröer, Rudolf Steiner is asked by Joseph Kurschner to edit Goethe's scientific works for the *Deutschen National-Literatur* edition. He writes "A Possible Critique of Atomistic Concepts" and sends it to Friedrich Theodore Vischer.

1883: Rudolf Steiner completes his college studies and begins work on the Goethe project.

1884: First volume of Goethe's *Scientific Writings* (CW 1) appears (March). He lectures on Goethe and Lessing, and Goethe's approach to science. In July, he enters the household of Ladislaus and Pauline Specht as tutor to the four Specht boys. He will live there until 1890. At this time, he meets Josef Breuer (1842-1925), the coauthor with Sigmund Freud of *Studies in Hysteria*, who is the Specht family doctor.

1885: While continuing to edit Goethe's writings, Rudolf Steiner reads deeply in contemporary philosophy (Edouard von Hartmann, Johannes Volkelt, and Richard Wahle, among others).

1886: May: Rudolf Steiner sends Kurschner the manuscript of *Outlines of Goethe's Theory of Knowledge* (CW 2), which appears in October, and which he sends out widely. He also meets the poet Marie Eugenie Delle Grazie and writes "Nature and Our Ideals" for her. He attends her salon, where he meets many priests, theologians, and philosophers, who will become his friends. Meanwhile, the director of the Goethe Archive in Weimar requests his collaboration with the *Sophien* edition of Goethe's works, particularly the writings on color.

1887: At the beginning of the year, Rudolf Steiner is very sick. As the year progresses and his health improves, he becomes increasingly "a man of letters," lecturing, writing essays, and taking part in Austrian cultural life. In August-September, the second volume of Goethe's *Scientific Writings* appears.

1888: January-July: Rudolf Steiner assumes editorship of the "German Weekly" (*Deutsche Wochenschrift*). He begins lecturing more intensively, giving, for example, a lecture titled "Goethe as Father of a New Aesthetics." He meets and becomes soul friends with Friedrich Eckstein (1861-1939), a vegetarian, philosopher of symbolism, alchemist, and musician, who will introduce him to various spiritual currents (including Theosophy) and with whom he will meditate and interpret esoteric and alchemical texts.

1889: Rudolf Steiner first reads Nietzsche (*Beyond Good and Evil*). He encounters Theosophy again and learns of Madame Blavatsky in the Theosophical circle around Marie Lang (1858-1934). Here he also meets well-known figures of Austrian life, as well as esoteric figures like the occultist Franz Hartman and Karl Leiningen-Billigen (translator of C.G. Harrison's *The Transcendental Universe*.) During this period, Steiner first reads A.P. Sinnett's *Esoteric Buddhism* and Mabel Collins's *Light on the Path*. He also begins traveling, visiting Budapest, Weimar, and Berlin (where he meets philosopher Edouard von Hartman).

1890: Rudolf Steiner finishes volume 3 of Goethe's scientific writings. He begins his doctoral dissertation, which will become *Truth and Science* (CW 3). He also meets the poet and feminist Rosa Mayreder (1858-1938), with whom he can exchange his most intimate thoughts. In September, Rudolf Steiner moves to Weimar to work in the Goethe-Schiller Archive.

1891: Volume 3 of the Kurschner edition of Goethe appears. Meanwhile, Rudolf Steiner edits Goethe's studies in mineralogy and scientific writings for the *Sophien* edition. He meets Ludwig Laistner of the Cotta Publishing Company, who asks for a book on the basic question of metaphysics. From this will result, ultimately, *The Philosophy of Freedom* (CW 4), which will be published not by Cotta but by Emil Felber. In October, Rudolf Steiner takes the oral exam for a doctorate in philosophy, mathematics, and mechanics at Rostock University, receiving his doctorate on the twenty-sixth. In November, he gives his first lecture on Goethe's "Fairy Tale" in Vienna.

1892: Rudolf Steiner continues work at the Goethe-Schiller Archive and on his *Philosophy of Freedom*. *Truth and Science*, his doctoral dissertation, is published. Steiner undertakes to write introductions to books on Schopenhauer and Jean Paul for Cotta. At year's end, he finds lodging with Anna Eunike, née Schulz (1853-1911), a widow with four daughters and a son. He also develops a friendship with Otto Erich Hartleben (1864-1905) with whom he shares literary interests.

1893:   Rudolf Steiner begins his habit of producing many reviews and articles. In March, he gives a lecture titled "Hypnotism, with Reference to Spiritism." In September, volume 4 of the Kurschner edition is completed. In November, *The Philosophy of Freedom* appears. This year, too, he meets John Henry Mackay (1864-1933), the anarchist, and Max Stirner, a scholar and biographer.
1894:   Rudolf Steiner meets Elisabeth Förster Nietzsche, the philosopher's sister, and begins to read Nietzsche in earnest, beginning with the as yet unpublished *Antichrist*. He also meets Ernst Haeckel (1834-1919). In the fall, he begins to write *Nietzsche, A Fighter against His Time* (CW 5).
1895:   May, *Nietzsche, A Fighter against His Time* appears.
1896:   January 22: Rudolf Steiner sees Friedrich Nietzsche for the first and only time. Moves between the Nietzsche and the Goethe-Schiller Archives, where he completes his work before year's end. He falls out with Elisabeth Förster Nietzsche, thus ending his association with the Nietzsche Archive.
1897:   Rudolf Steiner finishes the manuscript of *Goethe's Worldview* (CW 6). He moves to Berlin with Anna Eunike and begins editorship of the *Magazin für Literatur*. From now on, Steiner will write countless reviews, literary and philosophical articles, and so on. He begins lecturing at the "Free Literary Society." In September, he attends the Zionist Congress in Basel. He sides with Dreyfus in the Dreyfus affair.
1898:   Rudolf Steiner is very active as an editor in the political, artistic, and theatrical life of Berlin. He becomes friendly with John Henry Mackay and poet Ludwig Jacobowski (1868-1900). He joins Jacobowski's circle of writers, artists, and scientists—"The Coming Ones" (*Die Kommenden*)—and contributes lectures to the group until 1903. He also lectures at the "League for College Pedagogy." He writes an article for Goethe's sesquicentennial, "Goethe's Secret Revelation," on the "Fairy Tale of the Green Snake and the Beautiful Lily."
1888-89:   "This was a trying time for my soul as I looked at Christianity. . . . I was able to progress only by contemplating, by means of spiritual perception, the evolution of Christianity . . . . Conscious knowledge of real Christianity began to dawn in me around the turn of the century. This seed continued to develop. My soul trial occurred shortly before the beginning of the twentieth century. It was decisive for my soul's development that I stood spiritually before the Mystery of Golgotha in a deep and solemn celebration of knowledge."
1899:   Rudolf Steiner begins teaching and giving lectures and lecture cycles at the Workers' College, founded by Wilhelm Liebknecht (1826-1900). He will continue to do so until 1904. Writes: *Literature and Spiritual Life in the Nineteenth Century; Individualism in Philosophy; Haeckel and His Opponents; Poetry in the Present;* and begins what will become (fifteen years later). *The Riddles of Philosophy* (CW 18). He also meets many artists and writers, including Käthe Kollwitz, Stefan

Zweig, and Rainer Maria Rilke. On October 31, he marries Anna Eunike.

1900: "I thought that the turn of the century must bring humanity a new light. It seemed to me that the separation of human thinking and willing from the spirit had peaked. A turn or reversal of direction in human evolution seemed to me a necessity." Rudolf Steiner finishes *World and Life Views in the Nineteenth Century* (the second part of what will become *The Riddles of Philosophy*) and dedicates it to Ernst Haeckel. It is published in March. He continues lecturing at *Die Kommenden*, whose leadership he assumes after the death of Jacobowski. Also, he gives the Gutenberg Jubilee lecture before 7,000 typesetters and printers. In September, Rudolf Steiner is invited by Count and Countess Brockdorff to lecture in the Theosophical Library. His first lecture is on Nietzsche. His second lecture is titled "Goethe's Secret Revelation." October 6, he begins a lecture cycle on the mystics that will become *Mystics after Modernism* (CW 7). November-December: "Marie von Sivers appears in the audience...." Also in November, Steiner gives his first lecture at the Giordano Bruno Bund (where he will continue to lecture until May, 1905). He speaks on Bruno and modern Rome, focusing on the importance of the philosophy of Thomas Aquinas as monism.

1901: In continual financial straits, Rudolf Steiner's early friends Moritz Zitter and Rosa Mayreder help support him. In October, he begins the lecture cycle *Christianity as Mystical Fact* (CW 8) at the Theosophical Library. In November, he gives his first "Theosophical lecture" on Goethe's "Fairy Tale" in Hamburg at the invitation of Wilhelm Hubbe-Schleiden. He also attends a tea to celebrate the founding of the Theosophical Society at Count and Countess Brockdorff's. He gives a lecture cycle, "From Buddha to Christ," for the circle of the *Kommenden*. November 17, Marie von Sivers asks Rudolf Steiner if Theosophy does not need a Western-Christian spiritual movement (to complement Theosophy's Eastern emphasis). "The question was posed. Now, following spiritual laws, I could begin to give an answer...." In December, Rudolf Steiner writes his first article for a Theosophical publication. At year's end, the Brockdorffs and possibly Wilhelm Hubbe-Schleiden ask Rudolf Steiner to join the Theosophical Society and undertake the leadership of the German section. Rudolf Steiner agrees, on the condition that Marie von Sivers (then in Italy) work with him.

1902: Beginning in January, Rudolf Steiner attends the opening of the Workers' School in Spandau with Rosa Luxemberg (1870-1919). January 17, Rudolf Steiner joins the Theosophical Society. In April, he is asked to become general secretary of the German Section of the Theosophical Society, and works on preparations for its founding. In July, he visits London for a Theosophical congress. He meets Bertram

Keightly, G.R.S. Mead, A.P. Sinnett, and Annie Besant, among others. In September, *Christianity as Mystical Fact* appears. In October, Rudolf Steiner gives his first public lecture on Theosophy ("Monism and Theosophy") to about three hundred people at the Giordano Bruno Bund. On October 19-21, the German Section of the Theosophical Society has its first meeting; Rudolf Steiner is the general secretary, and Annie Besant attends. Steiner lectures on practical karma studies. On October 23, Annie Besant inducts Rudolf Steiner into the Esoteric School of the Theosophical Society. On October 25, Steiner begins a weekly series of lectures: "The Field of Theosophy." During this year, Rudolf Steiner also first meets Ita Wegman (1876-1943), who will become his close collaborator in his final years.

1903: Rudolf Steiner holds about 300 lectures and seminars. In May, the first issue of the periodical *Luzifer* appears. In June, Rudolf Steiner visits London for the first meeting of the Federation of the European Sections of the Theosophical Society, where he meets Colonel Olcott. He begins to write *Theosophy* (CW 9).

1904: Rudolf Steiner continues lecturing at the Workers' College and elsewhere (about 90 lectures), while lecturing intensively all over Germany among Theosophists (about a 140 lectures). In February, he meets Carl Unger (1878-1929), who will become a member of the board of the Anthroposophical Society (1913). In March, he meets Michael Bauer (1871-1929), a Christian mystic, who will also be on the board. In May, *Theosophy* appears, with the dedication: "To the spirit of Giordano Bruno." Rudolf Steiner and Marie von Sivers visit London for meetings with Annie Besant. June: Rudolf Steiner and Marie von Sivers attend the meeting of the Federation of European Sections of the Theosophical Society in Amsterdam. In July, Steiner begins the articles in *Luzifer-Gnosis* that will become *How to Know Higher Worlds* (CW 10) and *Cosmic Memory* (CW 11). In September, Annie Besant visits Germany. In December, Steiner lectures on Freemasonry. He mentions the High Grade Masonry derived from John Yarker and represented by Theodore Reuss and Karl Kellner as a blank slate "into which a good image could be placed."

1905: This year, Steiner ends his non-Theosophical lecturing activity. Supported by Marie von Sivers, his Theosophical lecturing—both in public and in the Theosophical Society—increases significantly: "The German Theosophical Movement is of exceptional importance." Steiner recommends reading, among others, Fichte, Jacob Boehme, and Angelus Silesius. He begins to introduce Christian themes into Theosophy. He also begins to work with doctors (Felix Peipers and Ludwig Noll). In July, he is in London for the Federation of European Sections, where he attends a lecture by Annie Besant: "I have seldom seen Mrs. Besant speak in so inward and heartfelt a manner...." "Through Mrs. Besant I have found the way to H.P. Blavatsky."

September to October, he gives a course of thirty-one lectures for a small group of esoteric students. In October, the annual meeting of the German Section of the Theosophical Society, which still remains very small, takes place. Rudolf Steiner reports membership has risen from 121 to 377 members. In November, seeking to establish esoteric "continuity," Rudolf Steiner and Marie von Sivers participate in a "Memphis-Misraim" Masonic ceremony. They pay forty-five marks for membership. "Yesterday, you saw how little remains of former esoteric institutions." "We are dealing only with a 'framework'... for the present, nothing lies behind it. The occult powers have completely withdrawn."

1906: Expansion of Theosophical work. Rudolf Steiner gives about 245 lectures, only 44 of which take place in Berlin. Cycles are given in Paris, Leipzig, Stuttgart, and Munich. Esoteric work also intensifies. Rudolf Steiner begins writing *An Outline of Esoteric Science* (CW 13). In January, Rudolf Steiner receives permission (a patent) from the Great Orient of the Scottish A & A Thirty-Three Degree Rite of the Order of the Ancient Freemasons of the Memphis-Misraim Rite to direct a chapter under the name "Mystica Aeterna." This will become the "Cognitive Cultic Section" (also called "Misraim Service") of the Esoteric School. (See: *From the History and Contents of the Cognitive Cultic Section* (CW 264). During this time, Steiner also meets Albert Schweitzer. In May, he is in Paris, where he visits Edouard Schuré. Many Russians attend his lectures (including Konstantin Balmont, Dimitri Mereszkovski, Zinaida Hippius, and Maximilian Woloshin). He attends the General Meeting of the European Federation of the Theosophical Society, at which Col. Olcott is present for the last time. He spends the year's end in Venice and Rome, where he writes and works on his translation of H.P. Blavatsky's *Key to Theosophy*.

1907: Further expansion of the German Theosophical Movement according to the Rosicrucian directive to "introduce spirit into the world"—in education, in social questions, in art, and in science. In February, Col. Olcott dies in Adyar. Before he dies, Olcott indicates that "the Masters" wish Annie Besant to succeed him: much politicking ensues. Rudolf Steiner supports Besant's candidacy. April-May: preparations for the Congress of the Federation of European Sections of the Theosophical Society—the great, watershed Whitsun "Munich Congress," attended by Annie Besant and others. Steiner decides to separate Eastern and Western (Christian-Rosicrucian) esoteric schools. He takes his esoteric school out of the Theosophical Society (Besant and Rudolf Steiner are "in harmony" on this). Steiner makes his first lecture tours to Austria and Hungary. That summer, he is in Italy. In September, he visits Edouard Schuré, who will write the introduction to the French edition of *Christianity as Mystical Fact* in Barr, Alsace. Rudolf Steiner writes the autobiographical statement known as the "Barr Document." In *Luzifer–Gnosis*, "The Education of the Child" appears.

1908: The movement grows (membership: 1150). Lecturing expands. Steiner makes his first extended lecture tour to Holland and Scandinavia, as well as visits to Naples and Sicily. Themes: St. John's Gospel, the Apocalypse, Egypt, science, philosophy, and logic. *Luzifer-Gnosis* ceases publication. In Berlin, Marie von Sivers (with Johanna Mücke (1864-1949) forms the *Philosophisch-Theosophisch* (after 1915 *Philosophisch-Anthroposophisch*) *Verlag* to publish Steiner's work. Steiner gives lecture cycles titled *The Gospel of St. John* (CW 103) and *The Apocalypse* (104).

1909: *An Outline of Esoteric Science* appears. Lecturing and travel continues. Rudolf Steiner's spiritual research expands to include the polarity of Lucifer and Ahriman; the work of great individualities in history; the Maitreya Buddha and the Bodhisattvas; spiritual economy (CW 109); the work of the spiritual hierarchies in heaven and on Earth (CW 110). He also deepens and intensifies his research into the Gospels, giving lectures on the Gospel of St. Luke (CW 114) with the first mention of two Jesus children. Meets and becomes friends with Christian Morgenstern (1871-1914). In April, he lays the foundation stone for the Malsch model—the building that will lead to the first Goetheanum. In May, the International Congress of the Federation of European Sections of the Theosophical Society takes place in Budapest. Rudolf Steiner receives the Subba Row medal for *How to Know Higher Worlds*. During this time, Charles W. Leadbeater discovers Jiddu Krishnamurti (1895-1986) and proclaims him the future "world teacher," the bearer of the Maitreya Buddha and the "reappearing Christ." In October, Steiner delivers seminal lectures on "anthroposophy," which he will try, unsuccessfully, to rework over the next years into the unfinished work, *Anthroposophy (A Fragment)* (CW 45).

1910: New themes: *The Reappearance of Christ in the Etheric* (CW 118); *The Fifth Gospel; The Mission of Folk Souls* (CW 121); *Occult History* (CW 126); the evolving development of etheric cognitive capacities. Rudolf Steiner continues his Gospel research with *The Gospel of St. Matthew* (CW 123). In January, his father dies. In April, he takes a month-long trip to Italy, including Rome, Monte Cassino, and Sicily. He also visits Scandinavia again. July-August, he writes the first mystery drama, *The Portal of Initiation* (CW 14). In November, he gives "psychosophy" lectures. In December, he submits "On the Psychological Foundations and Epistemological Framework of Theosophy" to the International Philosophical Congress in Bologna.

1911: The crisis in the Theosophical Society deepens. In January, "The Order of the Rising Sun," which will soon become "The Order of the Star in the East," is founded for the coming world teacher, Krishnamurti. At the same time, Marie von Sivers, Rudolf Steiner's coworker, falls ill. Fewer lectures are given, but important new ground is broken. In Prague, in March, Steiner meets Franz Kafka (1883-1924) and Hugo Bergmann (1883-1975). In April, he delivers his paper to the

Philosophical Congress. He writes the second mystery drama, *The Soul's Probation* (CW 14). Also, while Marie von Sivers is convalescing, Rudolf Steiner begins work on *Calendar 1912/1913*, which will contain the "Calendar of the Soul" meditations. On March 19, Anna (Eunike) Steiner dies. In September, Rudolf Steiner visits Einsiedeln, birthplace of Paracelsus. In December, Friedrich Rittelmeyer, future founder of the Christian Community, meets Rudolf Steiner. The *Johannes-Bauverein*, the "building committee," which would lead to the first Goetheanum (first planned for Munich), is also founded, and a preliminary committee for the founding of an independent association is created that, in the following year, will become the Anthroposophical Society. Important lecture cycles include *Occult Physiology* (CW 128); *Wonders of the World* (CW 129); *From Jesus to Christ* (CW 131). Other themes: esoteric Christianity; Christian Rosenkreutz; the spiritual guidance of humanity; the sense world and the world of the spirit.

1912: Despite the ongoing, now increasing crisis in the Theosophical Society, much is accomplished: *Calendar 1912/1913* is published; eurythmy is created; both the third mystery drama, *The Guardian of the Threshold* (CW 14) and *A Way of Self-Knowledge* (CW 16) are written. New (or renewed) themes included life between death and rebirth and karma and reincarnation. Other lecture cycles: *Spiritual Beings in the Heavenly Bodies and the Kingdoms of Nature* (CW 136); *The Human Being in the Light of Occultism, Theosophy, and Philosophy* (CW 137); *The Gospel of St. Mark* (CW 139); and *The Bhagavad Gita and the Epistles of Paul* (CW 142). On May 8, Rudolf Steiner celebrates White Lotus Day, H.P. Blavatsky's death day, which he had faithfully observed for the past decade, for the last time. In August, Rudolf Steiner suggests the "independent association" be called the "Anthroposophical Society." In September, the first eurythmy course takes place. In October, Rudolf Steiner declines recognition of a Theosophical Society lodge dedicated to the Star of the East and decides to expel all Theosophical Society members belonging to the order. Also, with Marie von Sivers, he first visits Dornach, near Basel, Switzerland, and they stand on the hill where the Goetheanum will be. In November, a Theosophical Society lodge is opened by direct mandate from Adyar (Annie Besant). In December, a meeting of the German section occurs at which it is decided that belonging to the Order of the Star of the East is incompatible with membership in the Theosophical Society. December 28: informal founding of the Anthroposophical Society in Berlin.

1913: Expulsion of the German section from the Theosophical Society. February 2-3: Foundation meeting of the Anthroposophical Society. Board members include: Marie von Sivers, Michael Bauer, and Carl Unger. September 20: Laying of the foundation stone for the *Johannes Bau* (Goetheanum) in Dornach. Building begins immediately. The third mystery drama, *The Soul's Awakening* (CW 14), is completed.

Also: *The Threshold of the Spiritual World* (CW 147). Lecture cycles include: *The Bhagavad Gita and the Epistles of Paul* and *The Esoteric Meaning of the Bhagavad Gita* (CW 146), which the Russian philosopher Nikolai Berdyaev attends; *The Mysteries of the East and of Christianity* (CW 144); *The Effects of Esoteric Development* (CW 145); and *The Fifth Gospel* (CW 148). In May, Rudolf Steiner is in London and Paris, where anthroposophical work continues.

1914: Building continues on the *Johannes Bau* (Goetheanum) in Dornach, with artists and coworkers from seventeen nations. The general assembly of the Anthroposophical Society takes place. In May, Rudolf Steiner visits Paris, as well as Chartres Cathedral. June 28: assassination in Sarajevo ("Now the catastrophe has happened!"). August 1: War is declared. Rudolf Steiner returns to Germany from Dornach—he will travel back and forth. He writes the last chapter of *The Riddles of Philosophy*. Lecture cycles include: *Human and Cosmic Thought* (CW 151); *Inner Being of Humanity between Death and a New Birth* (CW 153); *Occult Reading and Occult Hearing* (CW 156). December 24: marriage of Rudolf Steiner and Marie von Sivers.

1915: Building continues. Life after death becomes a major theme, also art. Writes: *Thoughts during a Time of War* (CW 24). Lectures include: *The Secret of Death* (CW 159); *The Uniting of Humanity through the Christ Impulse* (CW 165).

1916: Rudolf Steiner begins work with Edith Maryon (1872-1924) on the sculpture "The Representative of Humanity" ("The Group"—Christ, Lucifer, and Ahriman). He also works with the alchemist Alexander von Bernus on the quarterly *Das Reich*. He writes *The Riddle of Humanity* (CW 20). Lectures include: *Necessity and Freedom in World History and Human Action* (CW 166); *Past and Present in the Human Spirit* (CW 167); *The Karma of Vocation* (CW 172); *The Karma of Untruthfulness* (CW 173).

1917: Russian Revolution. The U.S. enters the war. Building continues. Rudolf Steiner delineates the idea of the "threefold nature of the human being" (in a public lecture March 15) and the "threefold nature of the social organism" (hammered out in May-June with the help of Otto von Lerchenfeld and Ludwig Polzer-Hoditz in the form of two documents titled *Memoranda*, which were distributed in high places). August-September: Rudolf Steiner writes *The Riddles of the Soul* (CW 20). Also: commentary on "The Chemical Wedding of Christian Rosenkreutz" for Alexander Bernus (*Das Reich*). Lectures include: *The Karma of Materialism* (CW 176); *The Spiritual Background of the Outer World: The Fall of the Spirits of Darkness* (CW 177).

1918: March 18: peace treaty of Brest-Litovsk—"Now everything will truly enter chaos! What is needed is cultural renewal." June: Rudolf Steiner visits Karlstein (Grail) Castle outside Prague. Lecture cycle: *From Symptom to Reality in Modern History* (CW 185). In mid-November,

112 * INNER EXPERIENCES OF EVOLUTION

> Emil Molt, of the Waldorf-Astoria Cigarette Company, has the idea of founding a school for his workers' children.

1919: Focus on the threefold social organism: tireless travel, countless lectures, meetings, and publications. At the same time, a new public stage of Anthroposophy emerges as cultural renewal begins. The coming years will see initiatives in pedagogy, medicine, pharmacology, and agriculture. January 27: threefold meeting: " We must first of all, with the money we have, found free schools that can bring people what they need." February: first public eurythmy performance in Zurich. Also: "Appeal to the German People" (CW 24), circulated March 6 as a newspaper insert. In April, *Toward Social Renewal* (CW 23)—"perhaps the most widely read of all books on politics appearing since the war"—appears. Rudolf Steiner is asked to undertake the "direction and leadership" of the school founded by the Waldorf-Astoria Company. Rudolf Steiner begins to talk about the "renewal" of education. May 30: a building is selected and purchased for the future Waldorf School. August-September, Rudolf Steiner gives a lecture course for Waldorf teachers, *The Foundations of Human Experience (Study of Man)* (CW 293). September 7: Opening of the first Waldorf School. December (into January): first science course, the *Light Course* (CW 320).

1920: The Waldorf School flourishes. New threefold initiatives. Founding of limited companies *Der Kommenden Tag* and *Futurum A.G.* to infuse spiritual values into the economic realm. Rudolf Steiner also focuses on the sciences. Lectures: *Introducing Anthroposophical Medicine* (CW 312); *The Warmth Course* (CW 321); *The Boundaries of Natural Science* (CW 322); *The Redemption of Thinking* (CW 74). February: Johannes Werner Klein—later a cofounder of the Christian Community—asks Rudolf Steiner about the possibility of a "religious renewal," a "Johannine church." In March, Rudolf Steiner gives the first course for doctors and medical students. In April, a divinity student asks Rudolf Steiner a second time about the possibility of religious renewal. September 27-October 16: anthroposophical "university course." December: lectures titled *The Search for the New Isis* (CW 202).

1921: Rudolf Steiner continues his intensive work on cultural renewal, including the uphill battle for the threefold social order. "University" arts, scientific, theological, and medical courses include: *The Astronomy Course* (CW 323); *Observation, Mathematics, and Scientific Experiment* (CW 324); the *Second Medical Course* (CW 313); *Color*. In June and September-October, Rudolf Steiner also gives the first two "priests' courses" (CW 342 and 343). The "youth movement" gains momentum. Magazines are founded: *Die Drei* (January), and—under the editorship of Albert Steffen (1884-1963)—the weekly, *Das Goetheanum* (August). In February-March, Rudolf Steiner takes his first trip outside Germany since the war (Holland). On April 7, Steiner receives a letter regarding "religious renewal," and May 22-23, he agrees to address the question in a practical way. In June, the Klinical-Therapeutic Institute opens in Arlesheim under the direction of Dr. Ita Wegman. In August, the Chemical-Pharmaceutical Laboratory opens in Arlesheim (Oskar Schmiedel and Ita Wegman, directors). The Clinical Therapeutic Institute is inaugurated in Stuttgart (Dr. Ludwig Noll, director); also the Research Laboratory in Dornach (Ehrenfried Pfeiffer and Gunther Wachsmuth, directors). In November-December, Rudolf Steiner visits Norway.

1922: The first half of the year involves very active public lecturing (thousands attend); in the second half, Rudolf Steiner begins to withdraw and turn toward the Society—"The Society is asleep." It is "too weak" to do what is asked of it. The businesses—*Die Kommenden Tag* and *Futura A.G.*—fail. In January, with the help of an agent, Steiner undertakes a twelve-city German tour, accompanied by eurythmy performances. In two weeks he speaks to more than 2,000 people. In April, he gives a "university course" in The Hague. He also visits England. In June, he is in Vienna for the East-West Congress. In August-September, he is back in England for the Oxford Conference on Education. Returning to Dornach, he gives the lectures *Philosophy, Cosmology, and Religion* (CW 215), and gives the third priest's course (CW 344). On September 16, The Christian Community is founded. In October-November, Steiner is in Holland and England. He also speaks to the youth: *The Youth Course* (CW 217). In December, Steiner gives lectures titled *The Origins of Natural Science* (CW 326), and *Humanity and the World of Stars: The Spiritual Communion of Humanity* (CW 219). December 31: Fire at the Goetheanum, which is destroyed.

1923: Despite the fire, Rudolf Steiner continues his work unabated. A very hard year. Internal dispersion, dissension, and apathy abound. There is conflict—between old and new visions—within the society. A wake-up call is needed, and Rudolf Steiner responds with renewed lecturing vitality. His focus: the spiritual context of human life; initiation science; the course of the year; and community building. As a foundation for an artistic school, he creates a series of pastel sketches. Lecture cycles: *The Anthroposophical Movement; Initiation Science* (CW 227) (in England at the Penmaenmawr Summer School); *The Four Seasons and the Archangels* (CW 229); *Harmony of the Creative Word* (CW 230); *The Supersensible Human* (CW 231), given in Holland for the founding of the Dutch society. On November 10, in response to the failed Hitler-Ludendorf putsch in Munich, Steiner closes his Berlin residence and moves the *Philosophisch-Anthroposophisch Verlag* (Press) to Dornach. On December 9, Steiner begins the serialization of his *Autobiography: The Course of My Life* (CW 28) in *Das Goetheanum*. It will continue to appear weekly, without a break, until his death. Late December-early January: Rudolf Steiner refounds the Anthroposophical Society (about 12,000 members internationally) and takes over its leadership. The new board members are: Marie Steiner, Ita Wegman, Albert Steffen, Elizabeth Vreede, and Guenther Wachsmuth. (See *The Christmas Meeting for the Founding of the General Anthroposophical Society* (CW 260). Accompanying lectures: *Mystery Knowledge and Mystery Centers* (CW 232); *World History in the Light of Anthroposophy* (CW 233). December 25: the Foundation Stone is laid (in the hearts of members) in the form of the "Foundation Stone Meditation."

1924: January 1: having founded the Anthroposophical Society and taken over its leadership, Rudolf Steiner has the task of "reforming" it. The process begins with a weekly newssheet ("What's Happening in the Anthroposophical Society") in which Rudolf Steiner's "Letters to Members" and "Anthroposophical Leading Thoughts" appear (CW 26). The next step is the creation of a new esoteric class, the "first class" of the "University of Spiritual Science" (which was to have been followed, had Rudolf Steiner lived longer, by two more advanced classes). Then comes a new language for Anthroposophy—practical, phenomenological, and direct; and Rudolf Steiner creates the model for the second Goetheanum. He begins the series of extensive "karma" lectures (CW 235-40); and finally, responding to needs, he creates two new initiatives: biodynamic agriculture and curative education. After the middle of the year, rumors begin to circulate regarding Steiner's health. Lectures: January-February, *Anthroposophy* (CW 234); February: *Tone Eurythmy* (CW 278); June: *The Agriculture Course* (CW 327); June-July: Speech [?] Eurythmy (CW 279); *Curative Education* (CW 317); August: (England, "Second International Summer School"), *Initiation Consciousness: True and False Paths in Spiritual Investigation* (CW 243); September: *Pastoral Medicine* (CW 318). On September 26, for the first time, Rudolf Steiner cancels a lecture. On September 28, he gives his last lecture. On September 29, he withdraws to his studio in the carpenter's shop; now he is definitively ill. Cared for by Ita Wegman, he continues working, however, and writing the weekly installments of his *Autobiography* and *Letters to the Members/Leading Thoughts* (CW 26).

1925: Rudolf Steiner, while continuing to work, continues to weaken. He finishes *Extending Practical Medicine* (CW 27) with Ita Wegman. On March 30, around ten in the morning, Rudolf Steiner dies.

INDEX

Abraham, 41–42
Achilles, 59
ahrimanic beings, 34
air, 46
   ancient Sun relating to, 17, 20–21, 38
   creative activity relating to, 21
Akasha substance, 2
Akashic Chronicles, 2, 34, 36, 45
ancient Saturn. *See also* Saturn
   condition of, 10–11
   existence of, 2–8, 13, 14, 17, 20
   time and space relating to, 8–10
ancient Sun. *See also* Sun
   air relating to, 17, 20–21, 38
   development of, 23, 33
   existence of, 17
   light relating to, 17, 20–21, 26
Angels of Beginning, 25
animals, 6, 71–72
anthroposophists/anthroposophical, 2, 6, 11, 61, 77
Archai. *See* Spirits of Personality
Archangels (Archangeloi), 22–23, 25, 26, 34, 44
art, 44–45
asceticism, 32
astonishment, 64–66
astral body, 33, 69

"being," Hegel's, 5
Being of the Earth, 27
Being of the Moon, 28
Being of the Sun, 26, 27, 28
beings, 11. *See also* human beings
   ahrimanic, 34
   concrete, 7
   cosmic, 69, 70
   courage-filled, 12
   free, 40
   higher, 48, 51, 66–68
   inner, 24
   luciferic, 33–34, 39
   of other hierarchies, 8, 33
   pure, 5
   sacrifice relating to, 46–61, 62
   spiritual, 15, 21, 30, 37, 47
   of time, 13
Beings of Will, 52
Beings of Wisdom, 52
bestowing, of virtue, 24, 27, 30, 34, 36, 44, 46, 62
birth, of space, 24
birth, of time, 10, 15–16
blessing, 19
Boehme, Jacob, 12–13
boredom, 53

Cain and Abel, 47–48, 67
Cherubim
   sacrifice renounced by, 34–39, 44
   Spirits of Personality relating to, 16
   Spirits of Will relating to, 9–11, 13, 15, 17, 19–26, 30, 34
   time relating to, 36
   winged, 11
Christ, 27, 42–43, 65, 73–77
Christ Being, 7, 26, 28, 73
Christ impulse, 27
Christianity, 76
clairvoyance, 4, 5, 7, 9, 12, 18, 77
coldness
   of cosmic space, 5
   Saturn relating to, 15
constellations, 76–77
cosmic beings, 69, 70
cosmic sacrifice, 15
cosmic space, coldness of, 5
cosmic system, evolution of, 1–2, 14, 33
cosmic warmth, 15, 30
creative activity, air relating to, 21

da Vinci, Leonardo, 27–28, 42–44
Damascus, 74
death, 69–78
desires, suppression of, 31
Dionysius the Areopagite, 25

Earth
   developmental stages of, 1–2, 14, 29
   Earth embodiment of, 2–78
   Moon embodiment of, 46–61
   Saturn embodiment of, 1–13, 30
   Sun embodiment of, 14–28, 29–45
earth, elements of, 70
Earth existence, 27–28, 63
Earth organism, 72
ego/egoism, 52, 54
Egypto-Chaldean era, 23
embodiment
   of Earth, 2–78
   of Moon, 29–45, 46–61
   of Saturn, 1–13, 30
   of Sun, 14–28, 29–45
enchantment, element of, 9
environment, of fear and terror, 4
eternity, 37
etheric body, 69
evil, 33, 40–41
evolution
   of cosmic system, 1–2, 14, 33
   human, 1, 26
   stages of, 62–78

fear and terror
   environment of, 4
   overcoming of, 6
fire. *See* warmth
free beings, 40
free will, 33

German psychology, 3
Givers of the Cosmos, 20
giving, receiving and, 22–23
God, 41–42, 47–48
gods, 37, 40–41, 78
Golgotha, sacrifice at, 6, 65, 74–76
Gospels, 1, 42
   of St. John, 76
   of St. Luke, 77
   of St. Mark, 77, 78
   of St. Matthew, 77
grace, 18–19, 26
Grantors, 20
Guardian of the Threshold, 3

Hebrew people, 42
Hegelian philosophy, 5, 12

"The Hidden Depths of Soul Life," 48
higher beings, 48, 51, 66–68
History of Philosophy (Schwegler), 12–13
Holy Spirit, presence of, 6
"homesickness," 50
How Does One Substantiate Theosophy?, 77
How to Know Higher Worlds, 6
human beings, 73
   astral body of, 33, 69
   deeds of, 30–31
   evil relating to, 33
   free will of, 33
   physical plane around, 2
   renunciation by, 31–32, 34, 37, 39
   resignation of, 32, 34, 35, 37–38, 41–42, 46, 62
   suppressed wishes/desires of, 31
   thinking activity of, 32
   will impulse of, 30–31
human evolution, 1, 26

"I," 2–3, 69
"I"-consciousness, 54–55, 73
illusion. *See also* maya
   of warmth, 15, 16, 63
imagination, 4, 5, 7, 8, 26
   as part of Rosicrucian initiation, 11–13
   sacrifice relating to, 16
immortality, 37, 42, 44
incarnation, 74–75
Infinite filled with Being, 5
inner being, 24
inner world, abandonment of, 4
Isaac, 41–42

Jesus of Nazareth, 65. *See also* Christ
John (saint), 76
Judas Iscariot, 42
judgments, 19

karma, 31
Kätie of Heilbronn, 59
knowledge, 64

Last Supper, 27–28, 42–43
light, ancient Sun relating to, 17, 20–21, 26

Living Time, 13
longing, 50, 53, 58, 60, 63, 66–67
luciferic beings, 33–34, 39
Luke (saint), 77

Mark (saint), 77, 78
Mars, 28, 43
material universe, spiritual context of, 29
Matthew (saint), 77
maya, 11, 14, 20, 30, 32, 38, 41, 62–63, 69–71, 78
meditation, 35, 78
Messengers of Beginning, 25
metamorphosis, 73
minerals, 6, 71
miracle, 65
Moon, 7
  developmental stages of, 1–2, 33, 66
  embodiment of, to Earth, 46–61
  embodiment, transition to, 29–45
  existence of, 13, 63
  heat relating to, 37
Mystery of Golgotha, 6, 56, 73–76
Mystery schools, 26

occultist, 43
"official psychology," 2–3
Outline of Esoteric Science, 1, 10, 14, 17, 20, 37

Paracelsus, 12
partial gratifications, 68
Paul (saint), 25, 74
Penthesilea, 59
philosophers/philosophy, 4–5, 12, 64, 65–66
physical body, 62, 69, 75
physical plane, 2, 65, 74–76
physical warmth, 17
physical world, 2, 78
pictures, 54–55, 63–64, 68
"planet of longing," 56
"planet of redemption," 56, 58
plants, 72
Plato, 75
post-Atlantean cultural epochs, 23
Prince of Homburg, 59–60
pure being, 5

realms
  of animal, mineral, plant, 6, 71–72
  supersensible, 76
  of true reality, 30
receiving, giving and, 22–23
redemption, 56
rejection, 34–39, 44, 62–63, 65–70
religions, 41
"remaining behind," 34, 39
renunciation, 46–47, 62
  by gods, 37, 40
  by human beings, 31–32, 34, 37, 39
resignation, 32, 34, 35, 37–38, 41–42, 46, 62
resurrection, 65
Rosenkranz, Karl, 5
Rosicrucian initiation, 11–13

sacrifice
  beings relating to, 46–61, 62
  Cherubim rejection of, 34–39, 44
  cosmic, 15
  at Golgotha, 6, 65, 74–76
  imagination relating to, 16
  rejection of, 62–63, 65–70
  relationships relating to, 67
  of Spirits of Will, 9–11, 13, 15, 17, 19–26, 30, 44
  substance of, 39, 44, 66–67
  warmth relating to, 10–11, 16–17, 34, 37, 46, 78
sacrificial smoke, 10–11, 25, 35–36, 38
Saturn, 7, 63. *See also* ancient Saturn
  coldness relating to, 15
  developmental stages of, 1–2
  embodiment of, to Earth, 1–13, 30
  spaceless warmth of, 15
  as state of warmth, 10, 14
Schwegler, Albert, 12–13
self-surrender, 17–18
self-will, 18
Socrates, 75
soul, 3–4, 12, 43
  life of, 16, 21, 29, 49–51, 55–58, 63–64
  milieu of, 26
  mood of, 17–18, 49, 53, 56
soul experience, 17

"soul theory without soul," 3
space
   ancient Saturn relating to, 8–10
   birth of, 24
   as ceasing to exist, 7–8
   cosmic, coldness of, 5
spirit, 46, 57
Spirit, Holy, 6
Spirits of Courage, 7
Spirits of Movement, 52–56, 58, 64, 67–68
Spirits of Personality, 10, 11, 15, 25, 26, 35, 54
   Spirits of Will and Cherubim relating to, 16
Spirits of the Macrocosm, 21
Spirits of Time, 10, 11, 21, 35–36
Spirits of Will, 7–9
   Cherubim relating to, 9–11, 13, 15, 17, 19–26, 30, 34
   sacrifice of, 9–11, 13, 15, 17, 19–26, 30, 44
Spirits of Wisdom, 20–25, 28, 34, 54
spiritual beings, 15, 21, 30, 37, 47
spiritual science, 18, 40, 44, 57–58, 60, 63, 71, 74, 77–78
spiritual world, 6, 31, 71, 74
The Spiritual Guidance of the Individual and Humanity, 59
streams/streaming, 9, 23–24, 26, 30
Sun, 7. *See also* ancient Sun
   developmental stages of, 1–2
   embodiment of, to Earth, 14–28, 29–45
   existence of, 8, 13, 20, 63
Sun beings, 68
Sun-existence, 28
supersensible realm, 76
surrender, 48–49

terror. *See* fear and terror
thinking activity, 32
Thrones. *See* Spirits of Will
time
   ancient Saturn relating to, 8–10
   beings of, 13
   birth of, 10, 15–16
   Cherubim relating to, 36
   as continuous, 36
Time Spirits. *See* Spirits of Personality

transformation, 73
true reality, 30, 62–63

universe, material, spiritual context of, 29

vertigo, 5
virtue, bestowing of, 24, 27, 30, 34, 36, 44, 46, 62
Vogel, Henriette, 58
von Kleist, Heinrich, 57–60

warmth
   cosmic, 15, 30
   deep nature of, 29–30
   element of, 10, 70
   illusion of, 15, 16, 63
   physical, 17
   sacrifice relating to, 10–11, 16–17, 34, 37, 46, 78
   Saturn relating to, 10, 14, 15
water, 38, 46, 63, 70
will impulse, 30
will substance, 47
winged Cherubim, 11
wisdom, streams of, 9
wishes, suppression of, 31
wonder, 64–66
"Word," 25
world
   inner, 4
   physical, 2, 78
   spiritual, 6, 31, 71, 74
Wundt, Wilhelm, 3

www.ingramcontent.com/pod-product-compliance
Lightning Source LLC
Chambersburg PA
CBHW050912160426
43194CB00011B/2378